Gyeongju

The Heart of Korean Culture

A UNESCO World Heritage

Gyeongju, The Heart of Korean Culture

A UNESCO World Heritage / Choi Joon-Sik. -- Paju : Hanul books, 2011

  p. ;   cm. -- (Hanul academy)
ISBN 978-89-460-5351-9 03900
911.85-KDC5
951.9-DDC21   CIP2011001512

Gyeongju

The Heart of Korean Culture

| **Choi Joon-Sik** | *Translated by Sandra Choe*

A UNESCO
World
Heritage

Hanul
Academy

Preface

Gyeongju, where Korea's most cultural sites are situated, is known to be the most popular destination for foreign tourists next to the capital, Seoul. Gyeongju is a meaningful place not only for Korean people but for the international community.

The city was the capital of the ancient Kingdom of Silla [57 BC-935 AD], which lasted for about 1000 years, the longest rule in Korean history. Due to the long period of its history, there are innumerable cultural remains all over the city. Buddhist vestiges make up the largest portion, among other things, since Buddhism was the state religion of Silla. For instance, both Seokguram Grotto, the one and only artificial grotto in the world, and marvelous Bulguksa temple are registered on the World Heritage List. UNESCO divided the entire city into five areas and designated it as a cultural heritage site and the city's more than half of historic remains are Buddhist relics. The fact that the whole city is recognized as World Heritage site proves an acknowledged status of Silla in the world. This is also related to an argument than Gyeongju was included into the world's four great ancient cities with Constantinople, Baghdad and Chang'an[Xian], which implies its high stature.

Despite the city's greatness, there are no in-depth books written in English that discuss historic sites and cultural relics of Gyeongju yet. It is so regrettable that I decided to publish books in both Korean and English. This is an English version. Here, I mainly focus on cultural remains inscribed on the World Heritage List, rather than covering everything with regard to Gyeongju. In addition, compared to the Korean edition, I revised contents that require too much historical background for foreigners to understand. Nonetheless, as the book fully covers the important places and cultural remains in Gyeongju, it will satisfy your curiosity.

Needless to say, I cannot imagine publishing this book without support from many people. I wish to thank them for their significant contributions here.

Above all, my greatest gratitude goes to Hanul publishing company. Humanities books are generally not very helpful in bringing in profit, not to mention those written in English. I once again offer my sincere thanks to Jongsu Kim, the chairman of Hanul, for his decision to publish the book under this circumstance.

I am also very grateful to Mr. Shin-Bae Kim, CEO of SK C&C, for his financial assistance to have this book translated into English. In Korea, many companies are not willing to provide the generous support for humanities research that was given by him. As he has refined knowledge in culture, he gladly offered me this opportunity.

Moreover, I would like to express gratitude to my former student, Sandra Choe who translated the entire text of this book. We could produce a high-quality translation of the book through deep discussions. I also thank my student, Nayoung Jung, for helping me translate some details.

I tried to show many photos in this book for readers. This was available thanks to help from many people. First of all, I would like to thank Mr. Guseog Kim, the president of Gyeongju Namsan Institute, among them. He made a valuable contribution not only to offering a large number of wonderful photographs of Mt. Nam, but also to proofreading the manuscript.

Also, I wish to express my heartfelt thanks to Ms. Bojeong Park, photographer Seyoon Oh who provided pictures of Seokguram grotto, and Dr. Byunghoon Min, the head of Asian Art department at National Museum of Korea. My students, Ms. Hyena Song and Seungjin Seo, deserve my sincere thanks for helping me in many ways. Especially Ms. Song helped in the collection of materials and drawing images, and Ms. Seo offered photos of many historic sites including Anapji in Gyeongju.

Last but not least, I owe special thanks to staffs in the editorial department of Hanul for their utmost efforts to publish this book. Without these efforts from Hanul, this meaningful book is not able to seen the light of day.

J. Choi Ph.D.
Seoul
Spring 2011(4344)

Foreword:

WHY GYEONGJU?

Gyeongju,
the cosmopolitan city

Whether in an international or domestic context, Gyeongju is an extremely important city. Gyeongju was the capital city of the well-known ancient dynasty of Silla. Silla lasted for an amazingly long period of 1000 years; this type of extended dynastic reign is a rare case that has few precedents in world history. Having been the capital city of such a dynasty, Gyeongju was able to enjoy a long lifespan of one millennium. Gyeongju was at its most prosperous during the eighth century, when it was considered one of the four great ancient cities of the world along with Baghdad, Chang'an and Constantinople. Today, Gyeongju is the least well-known of the four great cities, but this is probably linked to the fact that the national image of Korea is not widely recognized in the world today. But by being exposed to the relics and artifacts of Gyeongju in this book, it will be easier to understand why Gyeongju was such a worldly and sophisticated city in the eighth century.

It is a well-known fact that the Silk Road played a central role in bringing together the East and West in the form of trade and cultural exchange. The prevalent understanding today is that it began in Rome, passed through Central Asia via Constantinople and then ended in China at Chang'an[Xian], the capital city of the Tang dynas-

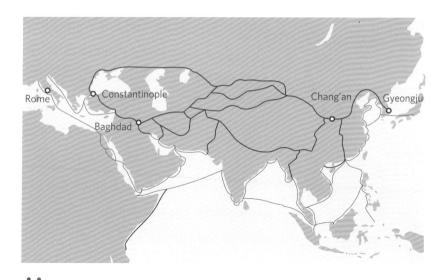

Rome Constantinople Chang'an Gyeongju
Baghdad

• •

Silk Road in the 7~10th Century

ty. But Koreans see it slightly differently; they believe that the Silk Road did not end in Chang'an but continued into Korea and ended in Gyeongju(Interestingly, the Japanese believe that the final station of the Silk Road was not Gyeongju but their capital city at that time, Kyoto!). Evidence of the cultural exchange that occurred through the Silk Road is readily found in the artifacts that are so easily excavated in Gyeongju. This point will be discussed at length later on in this book, but for better understanding of this trade phenomenon I will mention one brief example here.

Let us observe the bottle in the photograph. Scholars agree that this bottle has been done in classic Roman style. But it would be

●●

Roman glass bottle found
in one of the tombs of Silla
Kings
©National Museum of Korea

hasty to assume that this bottle was found in Rome — this bottle dates back to approximately the fifth or sixth century and was excavated from the tomb of a Silla king. Ancient glass is divided into Roman glass, Persian glass and Chinese glass; of these, Silla imported Roman glass in particularly large quantities. This bottle also most likely entered Silla via the Silk Road; Roman culture was a strong presence in Silla during that time. This issue will also be discussed later on in this book.[1]

From a Western perspective, it is easy to think of Gyeongju as having been a minor city on the periphery of the Eastern world, but nothing could be farther from the truth. I remember what a colleague who is a Silk Road specialist once told me. Let us say that there is a hairpin that was in vogue among noblewomen in Constantinople, one of the four great ancient cities of the world that was mentioned earlier. It would have taken only six months for that hairpin to end up in the hair of a Silla noblewoman. Many such items probably came into Gyeongju after a great deal of travel over roads and deserts, and a

• •

Central Asian statue found
in one of the tombs of Silla
Kings

fraction of these would have been sent to Japan as well.

    There are countless examples that show that Gyeongju was
indeed a cosmopolitan city, but let's just look at one more before
moving on to the next theme. The most representative case can be
seen at the royal tombs made during the eighth and ninth centuries.
Inside the many royal tombs located throughout Gyeongju, there are
often larger-than-life sized statues of people like the one in this picture. We can see that the face is not that of an East Asian. The large
nose and deep-set eyes are typical of a person from Central Asia.

13

According to scholars, this person was probably Indo-European or Turkish. Experts also point out that it was not at all difficult to see foreigners like this walking about the streets of Gyeongju.

Silla was actually very much a cosmopolitan country that had long since been a familiar name in the Arab world. Foreigners who are not familiar with Korea may think that Korea, nicknamed the 'hermit kingdom' in the nineteenth century, had always been re-clusive and obscure. But during the golden age of Silla, its prosperity was well-known in the Arab world; Persian geographer Ibn Khor-dadbeh's writes of Silla that "there is a land at the edge of China that has many mountains. This is Silla. It has a lot of gold, and Muslims tend to settle there once they have entered".[2] This book is probably the oldest foreign record of Korea other than those written in nearby countries like China and Japan.

Silla Culture:
The Origins of Modern Korean Culture

The capital city of Silla, Gyeongju, was without a doubt a cosmopolitan city. But Silla has a very important place within Korean history as a whole as well. Korea is a nation whose history is at least two millennia old. This 2000 year period refers to history for which records remain; if we were to include eras like the Bronze Age and the Neolithic Age that are accounted for only by artifacts, Korean history would easily span several tens of thousands of years.

Nonetheless, what is important to us today is modern Korean culture. No matter how long Korean history actually is, that history only has meaning if it speaks to Koreans living today; determining which period of Korean history is the root of modern Korean culture is an important question that they must answer. Modern Korean culture did not simply drop from the sky but is the result of past traditions that have been handed down. Under these premises, which dynasty can be said to have created the basic framework of modern Korean culture? The template of modern Korean culture as we know it today is Silla culture, which is what this book attempts to address.

Making that connection does not require a lot of effort — just looking at Korean surnames is enough. It is common knowledge to both Koreans and foreigners alike that Kim is the most common

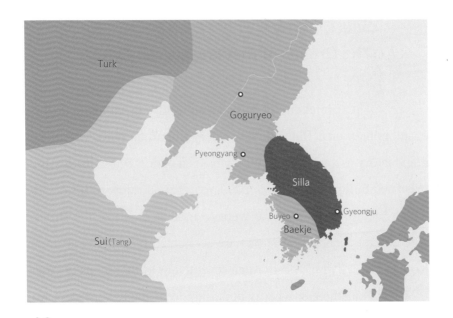

• •

Korean Peninsula in the 7th Century

surname in Korea. This is probably related to the fact that the Silla dynasty was ruled by people whose surname was Kim. Silla was actually established by a man named Park(which may account for the fact that Park is also a common last name), but most kings had the surname Kim. There are many other surnames as well as those that were created in later dynasties, but the majority of them have their origins in Silla.

Why is there such a phenomenon? This is without question because Silla unified the entire peninsula in the mid-seventh century. One of the most important periods in Korean history is the Three Kingdoms Period, which began in the first century BC as the three kingdoms of Silla, Goguryeo and Baekje. The following picture shows the respective territory that each occupied. As stated earlier, this situation changed in the seventh century when Silla forged an alliance with the most powerful country in the world at the time, Tang China, and defeated Baekje[collapsed in 660] and Goguryeo[collapsed in 668] in quick succession. For the first time, a unified country was born on the Korean peninsula and this became known as Silla.

The period that follows which is known as the Unified Silla Period is significant in various ways, but the most important of these is that Korean culture was finally centralized. Before unification, Goguryeo had a very cosmopolitan culture because part of its border was in modern-day Manchuria and it was thus influenced by northern Chinese culture. On the other hand, Baekje was originally established by Goguryeo royalty who had moved south to create their own country; Baekje culture was also as cosmopolitan as that of Goguryeo because of cultural influences from southern China. The Buddha statue in this picture proves just how highly developed Baekje culture was at that time. This statue created by Baekje artisans was sold to Japan before the seventh century and preserved there for 1000 years. It is currently a national treasure in Japan. Carl Jaspers, one of the foremost European intellectuals of the twentieth century, once praised this Buddha statue as one of the greatest religious statues in the world. As proved by this work of art, the culture of Baekje was one of the most advanced of its day; all of this would be transferred to Silla after the unification. The examples of Silla civilization that we will see throughout this book were among the finest cultural specimens in the world because they resulted from the amalgam of northern Chinese culture as absorbed by Goguryeo and southern Chinese culture as absorbed by Baekje.

•• The Maitreya Buddha Statue of Baekje preserved at the Buddhist temple in Japan

The thousand year empire of Silla continues until the mid-tenth century[936 AD] when it announces its collapse due to the new dynasty, Goryeo[Koryo]. 'Goryeo' is the antecedent of the English name 'Korea'; from a cultural perspective, Goryeo can be seen as an extension of Silla. Goryeo is then replaced in the fourteenth century by the Joseon dynasty-the state ideology shifts accordingly from Buddhism to Neo-Confucianism. Thus, culture that had been passed down until that point through a Buddhist lens was shifted to a Neo-Confucian framework. This actually has not changed very much since then; Joseon culture has passed down relatively seamlessly through the Japanese colonial period up to today. By looking at this process on a grand scale, we can say that Korea today has inherited the culture that was formed during the Unified Silla Period. When considering more specifically the remnants of Silla culture in that of modern Korea, the most significant of these is probably the linguistic similarity. Modern

●●

The Maitreya Buddha Statue of Baekje
©National Museum of Korea

Korean was created based on the language of Silla. As I have mentioned numerous times already, this is all because many aspects of Silla culture have been handed down to the present. The method of dividing Korea into administrative units of *gun* and *myeon* was also begun during Silla.

Another significant influence on the formation of modern Korean culture by Silla that is also the most easily verifiable one is that of religion, which in this case is Buddhism. It is not an overstatement that almost all of modern Buddhist culture in Korea has its roots in the Buddhism of Silla. Most of what can be seen inside Korean temples today are from that period. Of course some partial modifications have been made, but the basic framework remains that of Silla. First of all, consider the physical infrastructure of the temple — the buildings. Traditional Korean architecture is basically an altered version of Chinese architecture that has been molded to fit Korean taste. What is important here is that it was Silla that imported Tang culture. The temple buildings that are standing today are probably not too different from what they looked like during Silla. It is not only the buildings, however. When you enter the front courtyard of a temple, the first thing you will notice is a pagoda. The structure of all the pagodas found in Korean temples was fixed during Silla. Seokgatap, an eighth century pagoda that will be discussed later on, is the model by which the majority of other stone pagodas in Korea were created.

There is always a bell in the courtyard of a Korean temple; both the design and the sound that is produced have few equals in the world. This, of course, is in reference to those of China and Japan, who have similar Buddhist traditions. The greatest bell in Korea is without a doubt the 'Emile' bell at Gyeongju National Museum. This bell is recognized today as having the most beautiful sound in the world; it too was created during Silla. All bells found in Korean temples today were created based on the Emile bell. The same is true of the Buddha statues inside the Dharma Hall[Kor. beopdang 3)] of any temple. Buddha statues that are made today are almost identical to those of Silla. If you visit Bulguksa, one of the topics covered by this book, you will see a mid-ninth century Buddha statue that was created in Silla. It would be almost impossible for someone who is not an expert to differentiate this from the Buddha statue that is in Jogyesa in Seoul, which was made in the twenty-first century! There are many other similar examples, but these need not all be listed here. Although it is not certain due to a lack of surviving records, it is assumed that many aspects of temple culture like worship in front of the Buddha statue and sermon meetings were formed during Silla; these are conducted today in almost exactly the same manner. The same is probably true for Buddhist monk robes as well — the list goes on. But even what has just been covered on these pages should be sufficient proof that ancient Silla culture played a considerable role in the formation of modern Korean culture.

Heading out to Gyeongju

The cultural legacy of the Silla that I have thus far intro-
duced is all concentrated in Gyeongju. Thus, a trip to Gyeongju reveals an entire cross-section of Silla culture. In addition, one can
also see the original template of modern Korean culture by seeing
the culture of Silla; this is why Gyeongju is an essential place to stop
by for anyone who is interested in Korean culture. But there is too
much to see. Although many cultural properties have been destroyed
in the last thousand years amidst the changing of dynasties and frequent wars, there are still countless things to see in Gyeongju. This
is only natural, given the fact that Silla was in power for one millennium. Because it was such a long period of time, many cultural
properties were created and many of them have since disappeared.
But even so, there are still a considerable number that have survived.
Covering all of the remaining cultural properties alone would itself
take several weeks.

Thus emerges the question of how to properly tour
Gyeongju. The city of Gyeongju is divided into five districts that are
collectively called the Gyeongju Historic Areas and registered on the
UNESCO World Heritage List. Because these five districts are representative of Gyeongju, we will base our tour on what can be seen
in these districts. Just looking at the artifacts and relics in these five

22

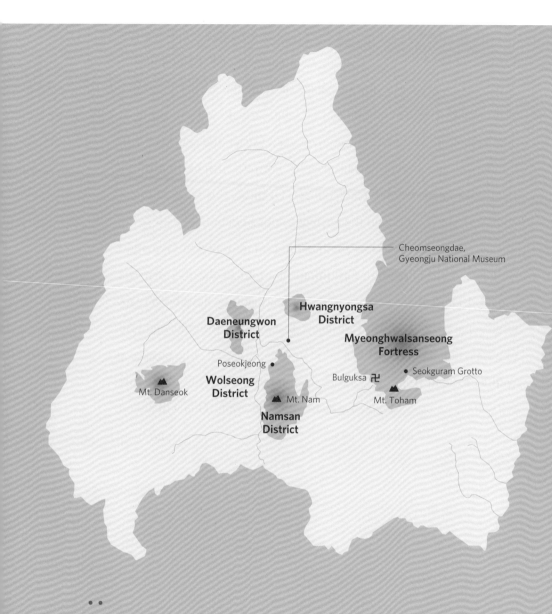

Cheomseongdae,
Gyeongju National Museum

Hwangnyongsa
District

Daeneungwon
District

Myeonghwalsanseong
Fortress

Poseokjeong

Wolseong
District

Bulguksa 卍 ● Seokguram Grotto

Mt. Danseok

Mt. Nam

Mt. Toham

Namsan
District

Gyeongju Historical Areas

districts can provide a good overall grasp of Silla culture. These five districts include: Namsan District, the treasure chest of Buddhist art; Wolseong District, the site of palace architecture of the thousand-year-empire; Daeneungwon District, where royal tombs of the early Silla kings can be found; Hwangnyongsa District, the center of Silla Buddhism; and Myeonghwalsanseong Fortress, the bastion of ancient Silla's national defense facilities. Of these, this book will deal with Namsan District and the ancient tombs in detail.

You may note that the most important relics of Gyeongju, Bulguksa and Seokguram Grotto, are not part of the five districts. This is because these two are so important that they have been registered separately as World Heritages. Just visiting Bulguksa and Seokguram alone will provide a good understanding of Silla culture as well as Korean Buddhist culture. Before going into the discussion, we will take a brief look at the history of Gyeongju. This will aid our understanding of Silla artifacts.

<u>1</u>

    The book 『Silla: Kingdom of Roman Culture』 by eminent glass specialist and Japa-
nese scholar Yoshimizu Tsuneo also provides further information.

<u>2</u>

    His book 『The Book of Roads and Kingdoms』 was published in the late ninth century.

<u>3</u>

    For all Buddhist terms(names of Buddhas, bodhisattvas, temple buildings), the
more well-known Sanskrit or Chinese term will be used. The Korean term, as well
as the Chinese or Sanskrit term in some cases, will be denoted in parentheses.

CONTENTS

❶ THE HOLY LAND
of Korean Buddhism, GYEONGJU

1. Seokguram Grotto:
The Prototype of Korean Buddhism

2. Bulguksa:
Realizing Buddha Land on earth

❷ A CITY of the 1000 Years Old Dynasty, GYEONGJU

1. In Downtown Gyeongju

2. Inside the royal tombs of Silla: The treasure chest of Silla culture

3. Mount Nam: The Holy Land of Koreans Past and Present

4. At the Gyeongju National Museum

WHAT KIND OF PLACE IS GYEONGJU?

Gyeongju is often called 'a museum without walls'. Not only are relics scattered evenly over the entire city, they can be easily found in whatever area you dig. There is probably no other city or region in Korea in which cultural properties are so heavily concentrated; there are 33 National Treasures, the most important type of relic, as well as 83 Treasures(several more treasures have been added just recently, so this number has probably increased by now). There are also 77 preserved historic sites, over 316 designated cultural properties and hundreds of old tombs.

As stated earlier, the entire city has become a world cultural property; UNESCO selected Gyeongju as a World Heritage item in 2000. We must keep in mind that it is rare for an entire city to be registered as a cultural heritage item. For example, Kyoto, the old Japanese city that is most similar to Gyeongju, has approximately 17 registered cultural heritage items. This is said to be an exceptional case. While the situation of Gyeongju is similar, the main difference here is that there were too many relics that qualified to be individually registered as cultural heritage items and so the entire city region was registered as a whole instead.

Also, we do not know just how many relics still remain buried. Old tombs, which will be covered in more detail later, are particularly relevant. If you go to Gyeongju now, finding an old tomb is as easy as finding a Starbucks in Seoul. It is that easy to see an old tomb because they are located just about everywhere within the city. Scholarly research indicates that there are many more relics still underground than those that have been uncovered. On top of this, an old tomb that has not already been damaged by grave robbers is sure to have relics inside it. The gold crown that is such a famous image of Korea today was also first found in one of these tombs.

The gold crown was first discovered in 1921, which unfortunately was during the Japanese occupation.[4] As enormous quantities of glass relics and gold crowns were excavated from the royal tombs, the Japanese government excitedly named Gyeongju an underground 'Shōshōin'. Shōshōin is an auxiliary building inside the Todaiji Temple complex in Kyoto that functioned as the storage closet of ancient Japanese royalty. The Japanese compared Gyeongju to Shōshōin because the latter stored the most precious items of its day. But how can Gyeongju be compared to a mere storage building? It would not be an overstatement to say that the entire city of Gyeongju is one giant treasure chest. No one can predict when or where the next relic will be brought to light.

It is estimated that Gyeongju at the time of the Silla dynasty was six times larger than it is today. However, it was not always so large; Gyeongju actually used to be a much smaller city. A 'city' back then was not like large cities today but was closer to a city-state. Originally named 'Seorabeol', Gyeongju began to acquire nation-like qualities as it conquered and assimilated neighboring city-states. One important point to note here is that the name 'Gyeongju' was not made during the Silla dynasty; the city was called by the common noun 'wanggyeong$^{capital\ city\ of\ the\ king}$'. The same is true for Kyoto, the name for its palace also being a common noun that means 'capital' and not a proper noun. The name Gyeongju began to be used during Goryeo, the dynasty that came directly after Silla, because this is when Gyeongju was demoted to be merely a provincial city.

Gyeongju began to look like a capital city as the country grew larger in the mid-fifth century. This is when city planning was first used. As can be seen in the picture, each section of land was divided into rectangular units 160 meters$^{approx.\ 525\ ft}$ wide and 140 meters $^{approx.\ 460\ ft}$ long. Because there were 360 of these units, called *bang*, the entire area of the city adds up to be a little over eight million square meters$^{1920\ acres}$. 40 years after city planning was completed, Silla decided on its official name in 503. The word 'Silla' is made up of two Chinese characters: the character *'sin'* means 'new' and *'la'* means 'to spread out far and wide'. The name is originally supposed to mean 'the king's benevolence is renewed every day and spreads throughout the land.' This is the point at which Silla formally becomes a country; the government then divided it into administrative divisions and established the practice of dispatching officials from

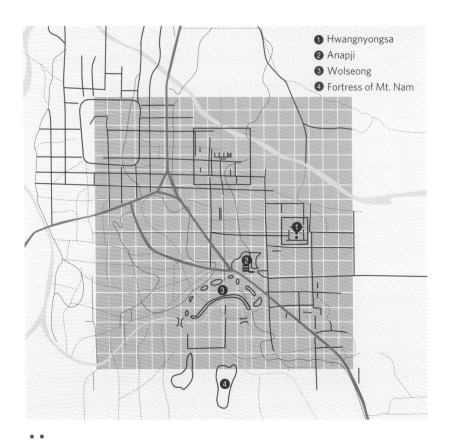

A street map of Gyeongju in the golden age

1 Hwangnyongsa
2 Anapji
3 Wolseong
4 Fortress of Mt. Nam

the central government. Gyeongju at this time began to be called Wanggyeong.

The central road in the capital city Gyeongju was the North-South beltway, which ran between Wolseong, where the royal palace was, and North Palace toward the northern part of the city. Only the site of Wolseong is left today, but this is enough to extrapolate that the palace was built in the southern part of the city. Building the royal palace in the south indicates a departure from Chinese architectural tradition. In China, it was customary to place the royal palace at the northern center of the capital city. Chang'an, the capital city of Tang China, was no exception: in front of it was Main Street[Zhuque Dalu], a broad street 150 meters[approx. 493ft] wide.

The people of Silla wanted to imitate Chang'an, the most cosmopolitan city in the world at that time. This is why they built another palace in the northern part of the capital, and a large road was built to connect this to Wolseong to match the Chinese style. But because Gyeongju was not as large of a city as Chang'an, this road obviously could not be built to the exact dimensions of its counterpart in China. Records show that this road was approximately 23 meters[approx. 75ft] wide; excavation results show that this road was divided into a pedestrian section and a section for vehicles. While the site of Wolseong still remains, nothing is left of the northern palace.

Of the various histories that deal with the Three Kingdom period, the one that is recognized as the official history — *Memorabilia of the Three Kingdoms* — writes that 'in Gyeongju there are rows of tiled roof houses and people cook rice using charcoal'. These tiled roof houses would also have included temples. There were over 200 temples inside the city gates at this time. Allowing for slight exaggeration, there was a temple after every other house; because all of these were stately and elegant buildings, the city would have truly been a sight to see. There were also dozens of buildings that were coated with gold and also ones that changed their appearance with the seasons: together with the temples, these would have added even more to the splendor and magnificent luxury of Gyeongju.

As with people in any place or era, a water supply was an absolute necessity; there were approximately 50 wells located throughout the city, which itself attests to the size of Gyeongju. It is interesting to note that all of these wells show traces of drainage installation, showing that the people of Gyeongju were living fairly cultured lifestyles. There are countless more records all indicating the degree of luxurious living in Gyeongju during this time that we cannot cover in this brief space, but even the evidence that has been mentioned should be enough to at least suggest that the citizens of Gyeongju were extremely well-off.

This ends our basic background introduction of Gyeongju, and we will now begin our tour. Because there are so many heritage items that have been registered with UNESCO, we must decide which of them to see first. Of all the cultural heritage items in Gyeongju, which of them is the most famous to both Koreans and foreigners? If Seoul has Kyeongbok Palace, Gyeongju has Seokguram Grotto and Bulguksa; books and pamphlets about Gyeongju often have either the Buddha statue of Seokguram Grotto or Bulguksa on the cover. This is of course because both of these heritage items are representative of not only Gyeongju but the Silla dynasty as a whole as well. Because these are registered under UNESCO, it is safe to conclude that they are important cultural artifacts not only within Korea but to the world as well. Having said this, let us begin our tour of Gyeongju with Seokguram Grotto and Bulguksa.

4

Also known as the Japanese colonial period, this refers to the period between 1910 and 1945 that Korea was an official colony of Japan. After the last dynasty, Joseon, collapsed in 1910, Korea was incorporated into what would become a massive colonial empire including Manchuria, Taiwan and much of Southeast Asia.

The Holy Land of Korean Buddhism, Gyeongju

SEOKGURAM GROTTO:
The Prototype of Korean Buddhism

It was the summer of 1964 that I visited Gyeongju for the first time. I was in third grade at the time, and I had been given train tickets to Gyeongju as the prize for winning first place in an art contest. I have been back to Gyeongju literally countless times since then: no other site have I visited more often for field trips and research. Although there have been so many trips after that first one, I still cannot forget the Gyeongju that I saw as an elementary school student. What I remember most vividly is the cozy and warm atmosphere of the city. This type of warmth is something that is rarely found in other cities, and I still do not know exactly why I feel this way about Gyeongju. It is something that most visitors to the city end up feeling; perhaps this is why the people of Silla did not move their capital city for 1000 years.

Of course, there is a more tangible explanation for why the Gyeongju that I saw in third grade is my best memory of that city. It was before development projects on Gyeongju began in 1971 and thus most of the original appearance of the city was still intact. In 1971, Korea was one of the poorest countries in the developing world with an annual per capita income of less than $1000; various clumsy development projects that were initiated during this time are responsible for much of the damage to the city's original look. Even after the destruction and damage that was done, if you go to Gyeongju today you will still be able to feel the atmosphere of the old city simply by looking at the remains. Had development not been done and the original state of Gyeongju preserved intact, I cannot help *feeling that Gyeongju would have been a beautiful old city equal to that of Kyoto. When in doubt about dealing with historic ruins, it is always best to simply leave them alone. Then, preservation work can be left to smarter future generations, but this unfortunately did not happen in the case of Gyeongju.*

Seokguram Grotto: Introduction

The reason that I am rambling at length about my childhood memories is because they are related to the path that leads up to Seokguram Grotto. It is a well-known fact that Seokguram Grotto is located near the top of Toham Mountain in the eastern part of the city. This thus requires one to hike to the grotto; while today there is a paved road that leads directly to the grotto and thus no need to go up the mountain on foot, there were of course no such facilities in the 1960s. We had to wake up at four in the morning and hike up the mountain. The walk took one hour; it was horribly painful at the time but now that I reflect back on it, that was the proper way to view Seokguram Grotto: it is the path that the people of Silla used for hundreds of years. Then, why do so at such an unreasonable hour? When I asked the adults while hiking why we had to go up a mountain before dawn in such a painful process, they would reply that it was to see the sun rise over the East Sea. I would then wonder to myself, 'The sun does not only rise over the East Sea. It's the same sun anyway — why do we go to see it simply for the fact that it's rising over the sea?' But because I was only a child and could not do as I pleased, I had no choice but to follow along.

By the time we reached Seokguram Grotto in this fashion, the sun would really begin to rise. However, it is difficult to see the sun rise on most days because of overhanging clouds. But the adults would simply repeat their mantra that we must see the sun rise and set out before dawn. It was only after I began to study Seokguram Grotto in college that I realized why one had to reach the grotto before sunrise. The reason is not directly related to the rising of the sun itself but the Buddha statue inside the grotto: I will explain this further in the main body of this section. In any case, if you follow the well-paved asphalt road up to the parking lot, there is a dirt walk-ing trail. The walk up this trail takes about ten minutes and is a very scenic one. The sunlight glinting off the leaves in the morning is an especially pretty sight. But it would be a mistake to think that the people of Silla reached Seokguram Grotto by this path because it has only been a few decades since it was created. It is a new path that was created solely to accommodate the massive numbers of tourists.

If you keep following the path, you will eventually reach

a large plaza and see a small house at the top. Most people probably expect to see something grandiose because it is a registered UNESCO heritage item, but this tiny structure is all that there is. What makes this small building different is that it houses a grotto wherein lies one of the most beautiful Buddha statues in the East. When you reach the house after climbing the steps, there is a door at the side where you can enter. The space surrounding it is always crowded because so many tourists visit here everyday. Let's now enter the house. Although you can enter the house, it is impossible to enter the grotto. This is because the grotto has been blocked by glass for preservation purposes. Because it is inside a cave it is always dark, but the Buddha statue inside is clearly visible. The moment you see it, you will be stunned by the breathtaking sight. It radiates a dignified yet compassionate aura. The cave in which the Buddha statue sits does not feel like it is of this world. It is a wondrous sight that cannot be expressed in words. You cannot help but wonder how on earth it was possible to carve such a soft and flowing appearance out of granite, a rock that is so hard that it is considered the most difficult type of rock to sculpt anything out of. Various thoughts will come to mind, but I think it is best to just observe without trying to think of anything at all. Isn't it enough for the best works of art simply exist?

Such thoughts do not last for long because of the constant

• • Miniature model of Seokguram Grotto

push of people entering the building. Even if you wish to stay inside longer, it is impossible not to be pushed out by the new wave of people coming in. Inside the grotto are not only the Buddha statue but also many other statues carved onto the walls, but there is no time to see these. On top of this, the innermost part of the dome is sealed off from public viewing so it is impossible to see beyond it. When I visited in 1964, not only was it possible to enter the grotto but I was able to touch each of the statues inside. Of course, this is unthinkable now. Now it is only a matter of ten minutes before you are pushed out again. People keep coming in, so it is impossible to stand one's ground against them. Because Seokguram Grotto is a world-class cultural relic, I cannot help but object to the extremely short period of time that I am permitted to view it. I have long since suggested that there be an information center at the grotto which can explain everything that there is to know about it. While it is understandable that entrance to the grotto itself is blocked for preservation purposes, it is an outrage that one has to pay an expensive admission fee to only receive several minutes of viewing time.

Today, computer graphics and other forms of information technology are highly developed and become more advanced every day. I suggest that an information center is created in which people can experience Seokguram Grotto via virtual reality. The structure of the grotto, the details of each sculpture and all sorts of other information about the grotto can be fully brought to life through 3D animation or hologram technology. After getting an idea of the grotto's general layout in the information center, tourists can then enter the actual building and mentally envision what they have learned even though they are not able to see the entire thing. This is probably the only way that the average tourist can fully grasp Seokguram Grotto; it never ceases to amaze me why no one sets about to do such an easy task.

The secret behind the structure of Seokguram Grotto

One of my colleagues who majored in architecture once told me that whenever he brings world-renown architects to Seokguram Grotto, everyone is at a loss for words. These individuals are more surprised by the architectural structure rather than the aesthetic beauty because they are witnessing the only artificial stone grotto in the world. There is no time for words because everyone is busy trying to figure out how the grotto was built. As can be seen on the blueprint, Seokguram Grotto is composed of two chambers: the front chamber is rectangular and the back chamber is round. The two chambers are connected by a corridor. The Buddha statue is in the round chamber in the back. It is this round chamber with a dome top that never ceases to astound architects. The fact that the dome was created by stacking rocks is a unique one. One point to note here is that the name 'Seokguram Grotto' is technically incorrect. This is because it is not a grotto at all but a stone room. A grotto is supposed to indicate a cave that was created either naturally or by digging out rock. But Seokguram Grotto does not fit into any of these categories. It is technically a stone room because a cave that did not originally exist was created by human efforts. But on first glance it looks as though it had always been a cave.

48

Why would the people of Silla have built an artificial cave? The practice of using caves in Buddhist worship comes from India. Because the weather is so humid, there needs to be a cool space for prayer and worship. A cave, which not only maintains a cool tem-

Structure of Seokguram Grotto

perature but is dark inside, is perfectly suited for religious purposes. This is why there have always been stone temples in India: the most representative ones are the Ajanta Caves and the Ellora Caves. This Indian tradition was then distributed far and wide via the Silk Road; Kyzyl Grotto and Bejekeulrikeu Grotto in Central Asia are representative cases of this. Grottoes of this type that are most familiar to Koreans are those in Dunhuang and the Longmen Grotto of China.

Silla also wanted to be a part of this long-standing Indian tradition. But the main obstacle was that the available stone on the Korean peninsula was of a completely different quality from that used in India or China. Rock that is found in India or China is sedimentary rock, which is formed when accumulated layers of dirt harden or when sand settles at the bottom of lakes. Thus, it is not

The Longmen Grotto in China

that difficult to dig it out to create a cave. There is even a case in India in which both the cave as well as the Buddha statue inside it were all able to be carved at once. This is how (relatively) easy it was to create a Buddhist grotto in India. But there was no such rock in Korea: there was only granite, the substance of which is so tough that not only is it nearly impossible to sculpt but even to simply dig out. Thus, preexisting conditions made it technically impossible to create a grotto. The people of Silla, however, after a great deal of trial and error with granite eventually decided to create a room out of the stone and then cover it on top with soil to create an artificial grotto. This was because it was considered theoretically impossible (and would have been an extremely back-breaking process) to actually carve out a cave from granite. This eventually became what we know today as Seokguram Grotto.

I have already stated that domes like this one are difficult to find in other countries. Not only has it been created out of 360 stone pieces, but the dome has been covered by more rocks with a top layer of soil as opposed to domes in other countries that are simply exposed to the elements. This was done intentionally to give the appearance of being a naturally-made cave. The makers of this grotto had to then go one step further to assure that the dome would not collapse under the weight of the additional stones and soil; it had to be built to be much stronger than an ordinary dome. For this, proficiency in highly advanced mathematics as well as the most cutting-edge technology of the day were both crucial. Even those who are not familiar with engineering will probably realize that it is no easy task to create a rounded dome out of rectangular pieces of stone as in the case of Seokguram Grotto. An entirely new type of technology would have been needed to support the added weight of the rocks and soil.

The solution was to drive in 30 wedges between the stone pieces, as shown in the diagram. In terms of physics, the wedges pull out the weight of the stones that would otherwise have pushed downward, making the dome much stronger overall. For the final step, a stone in the shape of a lotus flower was used to block up the top of the ceiling like a cap on a bottle. What is interesting about this stone centerpiece is that it is on the ceiling even though it is broken into three pieces. According to *Memorabilia of the Three Kingdoms*, the stone broke into three pieces in the process of lifting it up to the

Inside the dome of Seokguram ©Seyoon Oh

ceiling; apparently it was used exactly as it was in its broken state. There is no plausible reason for this, but what I find questionable is why the centerpiece was used even after it became flawed when the rest of this grotto is so perfect. A stone of that size could easily have been carved out again, but it is impossible to know why this was not done. In *Memorabilia of the Three Kingdoms*, the last section mentions that the architects were at a complete loss when the stone that they were trying to lift suddenly cracked apart. But even here there is no clear description of why the stone broke. Instead, the story goes on to say that one night while the chief architect was worrying about what to do about the broken stone, a god came down and lifted the stone pieces onto the ceiling. Although it is merely a story, we can deduce from it that the building process was an extremely difficult one. The stone centerpiece was probably so heavy that it somehow broke while being moved around and there was no chance or time to make a new one.

Even while enacting such feats of engineering magic, the people of Silla did not forget to consider the symbolism of each part of the grotto. The round room symbolizes heaven. The stone centerpiece that we just discussed symbolizes the sun and the halo behind Buddha's head symbolizes the moon. The stars are symbolized by the stone wedges. In this way, Buddha is seated in the center of the universe while giving a sermon to his disciples and bodhisattvas carved into the circular stone wall surrounding him. These bodhisattvas are not only on the lower part but also the upper part of the wall, each one in an individually carved room. With only the highest VIPs of Buddhism present, Seokguram Grotto is like a Buddhist paradise. We will learn more about the individuals here, but before that let us discover another secret behind the structure of Seokguram Grotto.

The amazing feat of natural humidity control

I have already reiterated that Seokguram Grotto was built with extremely advanced technology, but not all of it was necessarily scientific. This is because the forces of nature are also put to excellent use especially in terms of eliminating humidity and moisture. The most problematic aspect of buildings like Seokguram Grotto is the formation of moisture. This is unavoidable because it is an artificially created grotto on top of the fact that people frequently pass in and out. What kinds of problems accompany moisture? Moss would grow on the surface and result in erosion of the stone. Because Seokguram Grotto was built by royal decree, even more care was required for its preservation; even the smallest bit of damage would have been unacceptable. Nowadays this problem would be easily solved through the use of a dehumidifier or air conditioner. But how would moisture have been eliminated long ago when such modern technology did not exist?

Even Koreans living in the scientific age were only able to find the answer to this question toward the end of the twentieth century. The secret lies in a stream that flows under the floor. The Japanese who discovered Seokguram Grotto during the colonial period in the early twentieth century praised its artistry and skillful construction as 'unsurpassed by any in East Asia', and promptly be-

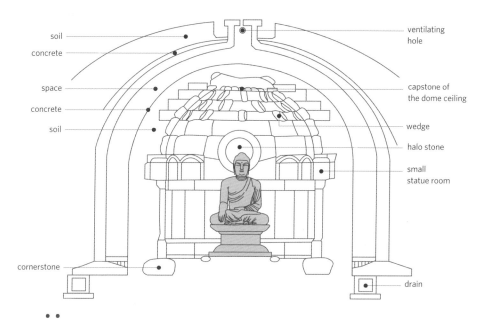

soil

concrete

space

concrete

soil

cornerstone

ventilating hole

capstone of the dome ceiling

wedge

halo stone

small statue room

drain

Cross-sectional diagram of Seokguram
after the renovation in a 1960s

gan rehabilitation work on it. What they discovered under the floor was a small stream. This was summarily blocked up, not considered to be very important. Cement, a high-tech building material at the time, was used to cover and seal off the top of the dome as a final step. Air circulation inside Seokguram Grotto became impossible. Predictably, dew began to form and this led to the growth of moss. As conditions worsened, the Korean government in the 1960s added another layer of cement over the original one. It then installed a dehumidifier. Entry by the general public was banned soon after-

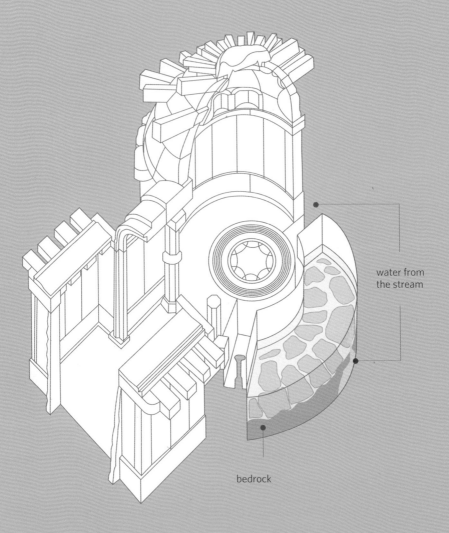

water from
the stream

bedrock

Three-dimensional view of Seokguram Grotto

ward, thus completely blocking off Seokguram Grotto from ordinary reach. Even with the use of modern technology, the problem of dew has still not been fully solved.

The solution that the people of Silla conceived was a humble-looking small stream. What does this tell us? What was a stream used for? The principle behind it is actually a very simple one. If a cold stream flows beneath the floor, the stone floor becomes cool. Then the moist air that forms inside drops to the floor as dew. Dew on the floor is not a problem because it is easy to clean up. Thus, moisture inside the grotto was eliminated by using this simple method. Both the Japanese and Korean governments foolishly covered the top of the dome with cement because they were ignorant of this simple principle. But using only this method would have been insufficient. There is no worry of moisture inside a building as long as air can be circulated. What sort of device was used in this grotto for circulation?

As shown in the picture, there are small square-shaped rooms lining the top of the inner wall that each hold a bodhisattva statue. This is where the circulation vents are located. These tiny rooms are not completely blocked up but have small openings at the bottom so that air can flow in and out. Do you remember what covered the dome? Remember that there was first a layer of miscellaneous stones which was then covered by a layer of dirt? Air was thus able to circulate freely through the spaces between the stones and dirt. Because the layer of stones was applied first, this would have been even more conducive to circulation because of the many tiny openings between the loosely packed stones. With these two methods, moisture was eliminated at the bottom and air was circulated through the top of the grotto to prevent moss from growing on the statues through entirely natural means. Seokguram Grotto was able to survive for over 1000 years thanks to nature-friendly technology.

Along these same lines, there is one more thing to investigate. If you visit Seokguram Grotto today you will see a Korean-style wooden building in the front section; there is some argument over whether this was built here at the time that the grotto was built. This building covers the top of the front room of Seokguram Grotto. Those who insist that the building was here from the beginning argue that without this building, this front room would have been fully exposed and it would thus have been impossible to worship inside it. Those who refute this argument say that the presence of this building from the very beginning would have obstructed proper ventilation as well as the lighting inside the grotto. While both arguments are correct to a certain extent, I think that this building was here since the grotto was first built. The biggest argument in favor of this is the fact that the space for worship would have been completely exposed without the building. However, the question that can then be raised about what was done about lighting inside the grotto is difficult to answer. Some say that there was no direct lighting but instead the stone floor was kept highly polished so that it would reflect sunlight, which would then naturally light up the room. Others like leading authority of Korean art Jon Carter Covell suggest that candles were used for lighting. The theory goes that the movement of candlelight would cause the sitting Buddha statue to look as if it were alive and the bodhisattva statues carved in relief on the walls to look as if they would walk right out. It is a highly interesting theory, but the questions surrounding this wooden building and the lighting inside the grotto remain unsolved.

Wooden building
in front of Seokguram

Going inside Seokguram Grotto: Appreciating unsurpassably beautiful statues

We have thus far had a basic overview of the structure of Seokguram Grotto. Now it is time to observe the little statues that are also inside one by one. Because we of course cannot actually go inside the grotto, looking at pictures to grasp the aesthetic and religious significance of the statues will have to suffice. Seokguram Grotto was built in the mid-eighth century at the same time as Bulguksa, and the same story is always told about these two structures. The prime minister at that time, Kim Dae Seong, built these at the same time for an interesting reason: Seokguram Grotto was built for his parents in his past life while Bulguksa was built for his parents in this life. As can be construed from this story, these two structures were not built for himself. This is because they were specifically constructed to justify the ideology of the regime. Looking at the duration of the construction work further proves this point. Having taken 40 years to build these two structures, the only institution at the time that could have provided continuous financial support for such an extended period of time is the government.

When Seokguram Grotto was being built, the Silla dynasty was at its peak in terms of cultural, economic and political power. This is the backdrop against which the construction of a grand project like Seokguram Grotto or Bulguksa was possible. It is said that construction of Seokguram Grotto was timed to match sunrise of the winter solstice. Winter solstice being the first day of lengthened daylight hours, it has a degree of religious significance as the 'great day that the power of light is victorious'. The Buddha statue was supposedly built so that it would be finished in time for it to receive the rising sun of winter solstice. There is another story that Seokguram Grotto was built to match the royal tomb[Sujungneung] of King Munmu. As the king who forged an alliance with Tang China and defeated the neighboring kingdoms of Baekje and Goguryeo, King Munmu was a Silla hero. It is said that Seokguram Grotto was constructed to face his grave as a tribute to his accomplishments.

But such architectural prowess is not the only reason that scholars today are in awe of Seokguram Grotto. While it is no doubt impressive that such technical skill existed so long ago, similar levels can certainly be achieved today as well. Then why is it that modern scholars are so amazed by Seokguram Grotto? As mentioned before, it took 40 years to build these two structures. The reason for this is not so much because the construction period was long but more due to the time needed for the planning and designing process. It was an architectural form that had never been done before, so it is only logical that it took a considerable amount of time to prepare for it. The construction of Seokguram Grotto would have been impossible without not only the skill of the architects, but also a high degree of expertise in mathematics, astronomy, Buddhism as well as an eye for architectural aesthetics. It is the combination of the elite of all of these areas that brought about the birth of a masterpiece like Seokguram Grotto.

What amazes us about Seokguram Grotto is not only the technical sophistication but also the aesthetic beauty of the statues that are fantastic and realistic-looking at the same time. A perfectly crafted Buddha statue and the bodhisattvas carved in bas relief complement each other. Also, isn't the dome-shaped area the perfect space to bring out the full beauty of these statues? This advanced level of artistry shows that the culture of Silla at that time was one of the most sophisticated in the world.

Ah! The Buddha With these thoughts in mind, once you enter Seokguram Grotto you first come face-to-face with the sitting Buddha, although there are many other statues around it as well. Because the master of this grotto is clearly the Buddha statue, let us begin with an explanation of it. But what kind of explanation could possibly be attached to this statue? Before we get into an analysis, let's first take a moment to just view it and meditate. Try to only think of one thing: remember the fact that this Buddha statue was made from granite. Granite is so hard that detailed sculpting is extremely difficult. Even one wrong hammer stroke can break a piece off. This is why an infinitely patient and meticulous touch is essential. Only such careful handling can create a statue that looks alive. An inanimate substance, rock, is given life by human hands. I stated earlier in this book that when going to see Seokguram Grotto, we always went at dawn. Now it is time to reveal why. If you reach the grotto just before sunrise, you need only a short wait before you can see the sun rise and light up the inside of the grotto. The Buddha statue, directly lit by the sun, at first shines brilliantly before it itself becomes a shining light. It is that moment that this Buddha statue is no longer a being of this world but is a heavenly presence. The sight of the Buddha statue when it is lit up from the center by the rising sun on the winter solstice is so fantastic that it defies all comparison.

You may feel that all of your problems can be solved just by looking at this Buddha. This is because this Buddha, having transcended all worldly pain, embraces all the unenlightened people standing before him out of his compassion. The people of Silla probably attempted to create what they believed was the most ideal image of humanity when making this Buddha statue. This statue is so perfect in itself that it is the model for all Buddha statues afterwards. This is why most Buddha statues sold in souvenir shops all throughout Korea are probably modeled after the one inside Seokguram

• • The Buddha statue of Seokguram

Grotto. In other words, this is the extent to which this Buddha statue has become engrained into the minds of Koreans. Of all the Buddha statues in Korea, this one is the most classically beautiful, but this does not mean that all Buddha statues found in Gyeongju are exactly like this one. Buddha statues made by lay craftsmen often look playful and even cute. The one in Seokguram Grotto probably has such a classic look because it was commissioned by the Silla central government.

After we have spent enough time appreciating the beauty of this Buddha statue, let us now turn our attention to its structural aspects. This statue is of Buddha when he called upon the earth god to defeat the devil. This may sound like it is from a legend, but this is not necessarily the case because it is a realistic depiction of Buddha on the day before he became enlightened. On the night before he becomes enlightened, Buddha is faced by one final test. This probably indicates his last struggle against the remnants of evil still within him. Buddha is tempted three times by the devil, who is trying to prevent him from reaching enlightenment. After having passed the first two tests, Buddha is tested one final time. His answer to this was as follows:

When the devil said to Buddha, "Prove to me that you are enlightened", whether it was out of modesty or the thought that the devil was not worth answering, the Buddha pointed his index finger to the ground. This was to bring out the earth god so that he could testify in the Buddha's stead. I am still not quite sure why the earth god appears at this point. The answer to this question depends on a thorough understanding of the hierarchy of Indian gods, but as no such research has yet taken place I cannot think of a concrete answer. Nevertheless, the earth god, upon receiving his order from the Buddha, promptly showed himself and proved that Buddha was indeed an enlightened being. This is the point at which the devil finally disappeared forever, and the story ends here. For those who wish to have a better idea of the situation, there is a good resource that I would like to recommend. Bernardo Bertolucci, the director who won an Oscar for his movie *The Last Emperor*, made *Little Buddha* in 1995. Whenever I lecture a class on Buddhism, I always show this movie when I get to this point in the course so that my students can see and feel the event for themselves. It is a method that is a great deal more effective than a dry lecture.

A close inspection of the Buddha statue will also reveal that the head is disproportionately large compared to the rest of the body, but this is an intentional distortion. It is because this statue was created for religious worship. It was specifically made so that it would look most natural from the place where the worshipper would be standing. Thus, the exact location of worship was the first thing that needed to be identified. As you can see in the diagram, the

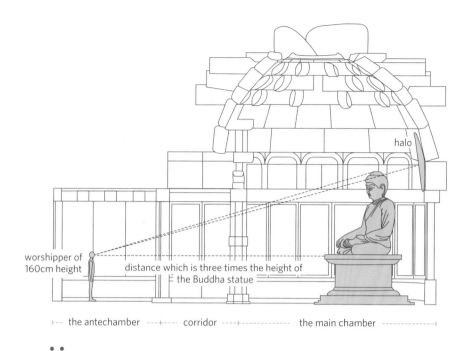

halo

worshipper of
160cm height

distance which is three times the height of
the Buddha statue

⊢--- the antechamber ---+---- corridor ----+------------- the main chamber -------------⊣

• •

Distance between statue and worshipper

exact location is a spot that is three times the statue's height away
with eye level fixed at 160 centimeters(approx. 5'3" – average height
was shorter back then!) above the ground. From this location, as the
diagram shows, the Buddha's head looks like it is at the center of
the halo. This provides the impression of infinite perfection. A halo
is the light that shines outward from the head of an enlightened individual. Religious paintings in the Christian tradition depict a donut-
shaped circle behind the heads of saints, being similar in function

Seokguram Grotto

to the halo. However, the halo behind this Buddha's head is not a circle but an oval. This was also done intentionally so that when the worshipper looks up at the Buddha from where he is below, it will look as though the halo is a perfect circle. In this way, we can see that the beauty of this Buddha statue is not only because of aesthetic sensitivity but extremely precise mathematical calculation as well.

There is so much more that can be said about this Buddha statue. For example, some say that in the process of building the dome, the Buddha statue was not brought in until after the dome had been constructed; instead, the dome was built after the Buddha statue was set in place. Others insist that the Buddha statue today does not look the way it did during the Silla dynasty, an opinion that requires some qualification. It is easy for people to think that the statue always looked this way. However, because it was commissioned by the king, there is little chance that the statue would have been left as plain, unadorned stone because this would have been synonymous with leaving the statue naked. Then what would it have looked like? Firstly, the entire body would have been coated with gold; color would have been added to the lips and other parts of the body. I once saw a television documentary in which the original appearance of the Buddha statue was recreated with computer graphics; the result looked extremely unnatural. I felt that the simple and undecorated appearance that it is today looks much better. But this can lead to endless discussion about the Buddha statue. Because there is still a long trip ahead of us, I will end my comments about this statue here and move on to the others in this grotto.

Circling Seokguram Grotto: In front of the Bodhisattvas

There are many statues of other people inside Seokguram Grotto, but the most important of these by far is the Bodhisattvas Guanyin that is located right behind the Buddha. Because this statue is completely blocked by the Buddha, it is impossible to see it if you do not enter the dome. Unfortunately, tourists and visitors are only able to see the front view of Seokguram Grotto and thus have no view of the inside. We too will have to be satisfied with this picture.

Of all the statues inside Seokguram Grotto, this Guanyin statue together with the Buddha is of the highest artistic quality. Perhaps the fact that it is the most convex statue in the grotto attests to this(the more the statue protrudes outward, the more difficult it is to sculpt!). It is also the most elaborately decorated. Why has it been sculpted with such care? It is because Guanyin and the Buddha are the masters of this grotto. Buddha and Guanyin each have their own role in saving this universe; the Buddha symbolizes wisdom, which is masculine, while Guanyin symbolizes mercy, which is feminine. Thus, we can say that these two are one body. Because they are of one body, the Guanyin statue is completely covered from view by the

● ● The Guanyin statue of Seokguram

Buddha in front of it.

People are captivated by the Guanyin statue because it so uncommonly beautiful. We must not forget that this too is made of granite, an extremely hard rock. But it looks infinitely delicate. While the clothing is of course magnificent, the beaded decorations of jewels that are strung together add another gorgeous yet finely detailed touch. As with the Buddha statue, Guanyin does not require further explanation. Simply being witnessing the artistry and technical proficiency for yourself is sufficient.

It is important to clarify here what exactly a bodhisattva is. There are many other bodhisattvas in this dome in addition to Guanyin. The word bodhisattva means 'being of wisdom', and these are not actual people but fictional beings. They were created with the rise of Mahayana Buddhism and are characterized by their sense of compassion toward all people. As Mahayana Buddhism rose to power in the first century BC, it emphasized love over the wisdom that one attains through meditation, the latter of which was emphasized by earlier forms of Buddhism. People who were hard-pressed to feed themselves day to day had no time to polish up their wisdom. There was instead higher demand for a god-like being that could provide assistance in hard times. Bodhisattvas were created to fill this demand. To that effect, bodhisattvas care more for people than themselves. Bodhisattvas are beings who have almost reached the level of the Buddha but have temporarily placed on hold their most important task — becoming a Buddha — in order to help other sentient beings to enlightenment in an act of pure self-sacrifice. They have extremely strong willpower, all in order to 'postpone entering Nirvana until there is no sentient being left in the world who is not enlightened'. What this really seems to mean is that they have given up on enlightenment altogether.

Another factor behind the formation of bodhisattvas is the increase in the number of Buddhists; as more people were attracted to Buddhism, it became increasingly difficult for Buddha alone to accommodate the prayers of all lay believers. More diverse objects of worship became necessary. Thus, the Buddhist clergy decided to divide up the powers of Buddha and then personified each one separately. For example, the most important of Buddha's abilities — compassion — is personified in the being of Guanyin. Within Seokguram Grotto, wisdom is under the jurisdiction of Mañjuśrī [Kor. Munsu Bosal]. After the formation of bodhisattvas, people who wish for compassion need only to direct their prayers to Guanyin. Because of these personal qualities, Guanyin is the most popular of the bodhisattvas for lay worshippers and this fact is duly reflected in Seokguram Grotto.

Notice that this bodhisattva is a bit unusual: you will see that there are many small heads carved into the space above her

72

• •

The Eleven-faced Guanyin Bodhisattva ©Seyoon Oh

head, being ten in total. Combined with the larger head below, this is called the 'eleven-faced bodhisattva'. Why are there 11 faces? One story goes that each face is compassionate, angry or smiling. If this is correct, why would Guanyin have an angry expression on her face? It is said that the anger here is not directed toward human beings but the foolishness and selfish desire that they possess inside. Making an angry face is meant to prevent human beings from having such intentions.

Another story argues that the ten faces represent ten different directions. Guanyin is known to have 1000 eyes and 1000 hands. She is supposed to appear immediately whenever a sentient being prays to her for help. Guanyin is like a 911 squad. The ten directions mentioned here refer to the four cardinal directions, the four intermediate directions between these(southeast, northwest, etc.) and above and below. This means that Guanyin is open in all directions. We can see how ardent her compassion is for human beings, and this is probably why she was the most popular bodhisattva. There is a bottle in her left hand: it is a water bottle, and there is a lotus flower in it. This water is probably not just any ordinary water but one that has medicinal qualities. In an area like India where the water is not very good, clean water itself could have functioned as a medicine. This water would also cleanse the hearts of sentient beings.

The lesser gods in the front room   This covers the most important parts of Seokguram Grotto. Now we will look briefly at the rest of the statues in order beginning at the entrance of the room. Too much information about only one part will result in not being able to remember anything afterwards.

The rectangular front room is a space for worship; it is filled with military individuals who are there to protect Buddhism. In the very front are eight gods known as 'palbusinjung' in Kore-

• •

Palbusinjung ©Seyoon Oh

an — perhaps the best English translation of this is 'lesser gods'. 'Lesser' indicates that it itself is not an absolute being but merely one among various other gods. In other words, it is a small god. There are various theories as to who these gods really are; one argues that they are assistants who protect Buddhism from evil forces and spread Buddhism to the people. This is why they wear military robes and either wear helmets or have animal heads. But where have these gods come from? The majority are gods that already existed in India before Buddhism was formed, and were quite important as well. By incorporating various Hindu gods as their own, Buddhism was probably able to present a familiar face to Indians. Placing these important Hindu gods in the periphery as mere doorkeepers was an act that Buddhists believed showed the superiority of Buddhism as a religion.

• •

The Diamond warrior ©Seyoon Oh

These gods are the lowest-ranked beings in this grotto; they do not have the large circular light behind their heads that the other gods have. This indicates that they are not very wise. Because of this, the least sophisticated techniques were used to carve them. This leads to instances in which scholars argue that these gods were added on by future generations. However, these gods are actually not as trivial as they may seem. Because we cannot see them all, let us use as an example the first god on the left, Asura. As a god who likes fighting, Asura was never regarded very highly in India; in Persia, however, he was promoted as the highest-ranking god. This is because Asura was very similar to the highest god in Zoroaster,

Ahura Mazda. The same god receives diametrically different treatment depending on which region it has been adopted in. In one place he is the best god^{Zoroaster} while in another place(Hindu or Buddhism) he is a god who likes to fight and is thus demoted as a lesser warrior to guard the gate of another master's house.

Right next to these eight gods are two threatening-looking warriors who guard the door to the dome. These two are called 'geumgangyeoksa' in Korean, the direct English translation being 'diamond warrior'. This name was probably meant to indicate that the warriors were as tough as diamonds in war. If you look carefully, their postures look like *kungfu* positions. Their faces and muscles on their bodies look extremely life-like. Note the bold lines of their abdomen muscles. They seem very enthusiastic about keeping evil spirits from entering the sacred space of Buddha. But although they are warriors, there is a round light behind their heads. This shows that they are advanced beings who are not only warriors but have wisdom as well. Then again, would just anybody be permitted to be bodyguards in the realm of Buddha? Another interesting point is that of these two warriors, one has his mouth open while the other's mouth is closed. It is said that the one on the left is saying 'ah' and the one on the right is saying 'hum', 'ah' and 'hum' being the first and last letters of the Sanskrit alphabet. This indicates that everything is encompassed from beginning to end.

Four Devas ©Seyoon Oh

If we now enter the corridor that leads to the dome, we can see the four Devas — beings who are very familiar to Koreans. When entering a Korean temple, there is usually a four Deva gate; although Seokguram Grotto is a very small temple, this shows that it is still fully equipped with everything that a temple should have. This is why some argue that it should be called a temple and not a cave. These four Devas are known as the guardian gods who protect Buddhism from each of the cardinal directions. Just as the eight lesser gods and the two warriors that we have just seen were all Hindu gods, the four Devas were Indian gods as well. They were simply brought over to Buddhism and given the role of bodyguard. Of course, they are not merely bodyguards but more like bodyguard chiefs. This was again probably an intentional tactic intended to attract Indians to Buddhism by using familiar faces. We can also see the elitist men-

● ●

Buddha status seen from antechamber

tality that even high-ranking gods in Hinduism are only fit to be lesser warriors when they are adopted into Buddhism. However, one strange inconsistency is that as a religion that values compassion, the evil demons that are crushed under the heel of the Devas look rather pitiful, considering that the demons are also sentient beings that should be pitied rather than senselessly stepped on. These Devas are said to originally have been in color, but it has all since peeled away and only the bare stone remains.

Just before the four Devas are two octagonal columns. The

fact that they are octagonal refers to the Noble Eightfold Paths, the most basic tenet of Buddhism. The Noble Eightfold Paths refer to the eight proper methods of meditation; the first of these is '*jeong-gyeon*', which would be translated into 'right understanding' in English. This shows that Buddhism is a religion that considers understanding and realization to be the most important above all. Among the noble eightfold paths, none emphasize faith more than the path of 'right faith [belief].' Buddhists believe that after you become truly free after having realized the truth, it is no longer necessary to believe in any tenets.

Disciples and Bodhisattvas: Those who praise Buddha   **Once** you enter the dome, a Buddhist utopia awaits. The most important beings in Buddhism are all gathered here. Because these have also been crafted by world-class sculptors, it is like entering a pure fantasy world. Here there are four godly beings and ten actual people. The ten actual people were disciples of the living Buddha.

Just as you enter, you will find on your left and right Indra and Brahma — who are these gods? Brahma is the Indian god who created the world and is also the highest god in Hinduism. Indra is the god of thunder and lightning who is also the most important god in the Hindu scripture *Rig Veda*. They are basically the two most important gods in Hinduism, but Indra and Brahma have not only been

incorporated by Buddhism but demoted as assistants of Buddha who can do nothing but praise him from below.

Next to these are Mañjuśrí and Samantabhadra [Kor. Bohyeon Bosal], the two most important bodhisattvas after Guanyin. As with Buddha and Guanyin, these four statues were also made with the finest craftsmanship available; although they are perhaps less elaborate than Guanyin, the level of the sculpting seems to have been consistent. Again, one is amazed by the level of fine detail considering the fact that they are all granite; they are exquisite while also giving the impression on fullness. No further words are needed to describe these statues. Anyone with even a mild aesthetic sense will automatically recognize that they are uncommonly beautiful. But these two bodhisattvas are slightly different from Indra and Brahma: the haloes of the Hindu gods look slightly different from those of the others. The haloes of the others are all circular, while those of the Hindu gods are shaped like upside-down eggs. The reason for this is unclear but the difference is probably due to the fact that the Hindu gods are heavenly gods. The two bodhisattvas each represent different virtues of the Buddha: Mañjuśrí symbolizes wisdom while Samantabhadra symbolizes the everyday practice of theory. This does not mean that they are not compassionate. Bodhisattvas have all the qualities of Buddha; the only difference is that each has a slightly different area of specialty.

The next statues to turn our attention to are the ten disciples of Buddha. While Buddha had countless disciples in his lifetime including his aunt and wife, these are the ten who were the closest to him. They were all real individuals. The only ones in this grotto who actually lived in this world are Buddha and his ten disciples. The rest are all bodhisattvas or gods who only exist inside people's hearts or in paradise. Perhaps it is because they were ascetics, but all of Buddha's disciples are sculpted in a very simple style. There are no other decorations apart from their religious robes. There are many stories about the disciples. While we cannot cover them all due to lack of space, let's go over a few of the more interesting ones.

When directly facing Guanyin, the figure directly to the right of the Buddha is Rāhula. Rāhula is Buddha's son who was born before Buddha left home, but he eventually became his father's disciple and rose to an important position within the priesthood. Although Buddha technically no longer had connections to his family after leaving them, he did not turn his back on them entirely. It may look as though Buddhism only considers life after entering the priesthood important and does not place any emphasis on the life prior to that. This is why many Buddhist monks do not even attend their parents' funeral. But Buddha was different. Not only did he ac-

Rāhula in the middle
©Seyoon Oh

cept his son as his disciple but also his wife and the aunt who raised him as well; in this way, he ended up saving the family members who were closest to him. Although Buddha had abandoned all concept of family, it is interesting to wonder how he would have treated his son Rāhula. One interesting point is that Rāhula was given a stern word of advice by the elders of the priesthood. The basic message was that 'although your father may be our teacher, do not count on the fact that you are our teacher's son'. Surely Buddha would have realized that bringing his son into his organization would cause these types of problems; I wonder how it is that Buddha gave Rāhula permission to enter the priesthood.

The monk third to the left of Rāhula is noticeably advanced in age; this is Buddha's prize disciple Kasyapa. Kasyapa took charge of the organization after Buddha passed away; he may have been depicted as an old man to emphasize this aspect and in fact may not have been elderly at all. He is on a similar plane as the disciple Peter in Christianity, but in terms of importance may be closer to Paul because he is the one who created the foundations of early Buddhism. Kasyapa played a central role not only at Buddha's funeral but also when editing and compiling Buddha's words into scripture.

Considering this, the monk to the left of Guanyin looks to be the youngest of the ten disciples — although he could not have been younger than Rāhula! — this is Ananda, who was Buddha's personal attendant for his entire life. It is said that Ananda was Buddha's cousin, so the two would have had a very close relationship on many levels. Because he spent his entire life with Buddha, he heard the most of Buddha's sermons out of all the disciples. This is why when the disciples were editing Buddha's teachings after his death, they relied the most on Ananda. Buddha's teachings were organized and compiled in the following fashion: when Ananda said 'This is what I have heard(from Buddha)', the other disciples listening close by would agree. If you look at Buddhist scriptures, the text always begins with 'This is what I have heard': it is based on actual historical circumstances.

•• Kasyapa in the middle

•• Anada in the middle ©Seyoon Oh

Going through each disciple one by one in this fashion could go on endlessly because there is so much to say. For example, the disciple right next to Rāhula went blind because he trained without sleeping after being chastised by the Buddha for dozing off once while meditating. Of course, he eventually becomes enlightened through such harsh training. On a different note, two of Buddha's disciples pass away earlier than the Buddha. It is said afterwards that Buddha always carried seat cushions for these two disciples wherever he went and placed them out empty in order to remember them. This episode is often quoted when arguing that even enlightened individuals also feel human emotions. For Buddha, his disciples were like his children; the death of two of them would have been devastating.

The last part to see are the small statue rooms that line the top of the dome. There are ten rooms with a statue placed inside each

● ●

The statue of
Vimalakirti
©Seyoon Oh

one. Creating rooms like these is a tradition that is borrowed from India, but it is said that few of the rooms are actually built to scale like Seokguram Grotto. Most of the statues are sitting bodhisattvas, but two of them are missing. Koreans believe that because they disappeared during the Japanese colonial period they were somehow sent over to Japan. There is much to say about these statues as well, but because we have already discussed bodhisattvas at length let us just go over one interesting point. The bodhisattva in the room directly left of the Buddha is sculpted in a unique manner. The statues that we have seen in Seokguram Grotto thus far are all highly exquisite. This one, however, is sculpted in a very rough manner. It goes as far as to look unfinished, but the reason behind this is unknown.

This is actually not a bodhisattva. It is a lay believer named Vimalakīrti; in Mahayana Buddhism, there is even a scripture named after him — *Vimalakīrti Sutra* — and he is the most famous lay Buddhist. However, he was not a real individual. If you read this scripture, there is a scene in which Vimalakīrti has a discussion with Mañjuśrī, the wisest bodhisattva, about truth. He then receives the highest of compliments from Mañjuśrī. Seokguram Grotto clearly reflects this relationship; they are on either side of each other and are debating with each other the nature of the highest truth. But even with such a layout, it is still impossible to understand why Vimalakīrti has been sculpted so roughly. One guess is that this was not an accident and that there is definitely an explanation for it.

Leaving Seokguram Grotto   We have now had a good general overview of Seokguram Grotto. It may have been only an overview but we have actually managed to see a lot. To that effect, even a full-length book would not be enough for a serious study of this grotto. We will have few opportunities in the rest of this tour to inspect a cultural relic in this much detail with the exception of Bulguksa. This shows that Seokguram Grotto is that important of a relic.

On your way back down the steps while recalling the advanced religiosity, artistic sophistication and high level of science of Seokguram Grotto, you will notice a pile of stones used for building. These have definitely come from the grotto, but their exact purpose is unknown. The fact that this rock is still lying around indicates that the restoration of Seokguram Grotto is still incomplete. It is a consequence of the fact that the Japanese colonial government was not fully prepared when it began reconstruction on the grotto in the early twentieth century. Research on the grotto was unfinished and the available technical skill was not very good quality, but reconstruction work was nonetheless pushed through. Because the work was not properly done at that time, it is difficult now to reestablish its original appearance.

However, there is still hope; if more research is done and technology improves, Seokguram Grotto may still have a chance of being fully restored. The most urgent task is the removal of the cement layer on the dome but it is being approached with caution. The rationale is that hasty decisions may harm the stones that make up the dome roof, but this process can probably be done without too much difficulty if technology improves in the near future. With these thoughts in mind, let's go back down the mountain path and return to the parking lot. I always feel regret when leaving behind Seokguram Grotto because I have not had sufficient time to really appreciate and feel from the bottom of my heart this great work of art. The time permitted is too short and the viewing space is not large enough. All we can do is take solace in the fact that we have actually viewed one of the finest Buddha statues in the world and relive that indescribable form in our thoughts. The next destination is, as always, Bulguksa.

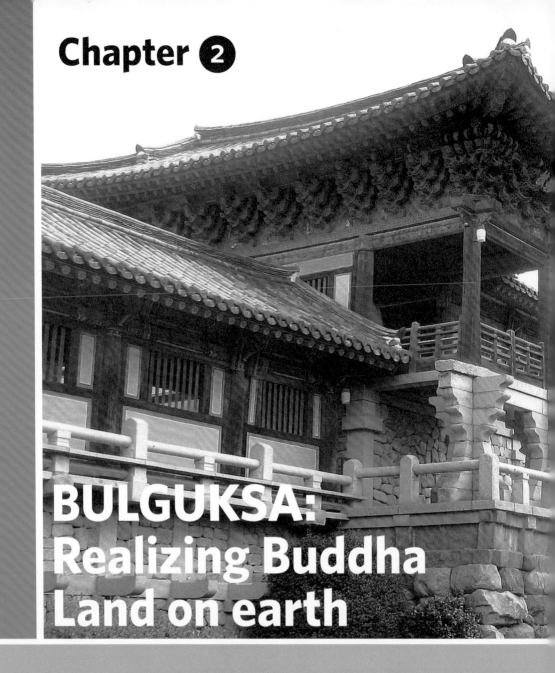

Chapter ❷

BULGUKSA: Realizing Buddha Land on earth

Before entering Bulguksa [5)]

Why was Bulguksa built?   Stopping by at Bulguksa after Seokguram Grotto is a required course of any school field trip. These two are always done together. Most people, as for Seokguram Grotto, simply get off the bus, take a quick glance around, and then are back on the bus to go to the next destination. However, this is not a casual tourist attraction because there are so many aspects of this temple to see and understand. It is no ordinary temple. Although it may look like one to the untrained eye, it is the outcome of a prolonged campaign by the Silla government 1300 years ago and is thus unlike any other temple. Silla at that time was one of the most developed nations in the world. A temple that was funded and supported by such a government is sure to be an extraordinary spectacle.

But this temple does not look so special today. If you stand facing the front of the temple, the view is not all that beautiful. A major temple that received financial support from the Silla government, one of the most advanced nations of its day, should have some sort of visual feature that moves the heart of whoever lays eyes on it. However, no such feature exists today. This is because modern Koreans have not properly restored Bulguksa. Proper renovation work would have rendered this temple several times more beautiful than it is. Known by only a few specialists in this area, not even the monks who live here are fully aware of the situation; even if they do know what the temple really could have looked like, there does not seem to be any interest in putting this into action. It is thus a question of whether this temple will ever be able to recover its original dignity and grandeur.

There is a story that is always told by the cultural tour guides here and books about Bulguksa. As with Seokguram Grotto, it is said that the prime minister who was in office while this temple was being built gave orders for its construction so that he could use it to honor his parents; there is also the story that the prime minister had the temple designed according to the principles of Huayan ^{Kor. Hwaeom} Buddhism. This cliché explanation is not that necessary; what is important is not this type of highbrow background information but an explanation of why this temple is outstanding from an artistic or religious perspec-

tive. Unfortunately, over half of what is explained to visitors today consists of a tired rendition of facts about the past that all sound the same. A straight recounting of the past cannot explain why this tem-

● ●

An Overview of Bulguksa

ple is a World Heritage item today: this will be the focus of our tour of Bulguksa in this book. The point of this explanation will be the reason why the religious and aesthetic aspects of the temple qualify it to be a registered world cultural heritage. For more background information about the history of Bulguksa and the complexities of Buddhist doctrine, I would recommend that you go to other relevant books on those topics.

I have firmly declared that I will not delve into background explanation; however, there is one point that cannot avoid mention. This has to do with why the Silla government at that time decided to construct Bulguksa in the first place. The characters 'Bulguk' in the name 'Bulguksa' mean 'country of Buddha'. Thus, this temple was built in the country(Buddhist paradise) where Buddha reigns supreme. Why did the Silla ruling class attempt to build such a temple? Members of Silla royalty believed that Silla was truly a country of the Buddha. They thus also believed that long ago, Buddhas actually lived in Silla. This actually does not go counter to established Buddhist doctrine, which also states that there were countless Buddhas before Śākyamuni Buddha lived.

Therefore, Silla becomes a holy land because it has been home to so many Buddhas. Also, the king who rules over the Buddha land of Silla himself becomes a Buddha by default because only a Buddha can govern a Buddha land. As did several Chinese emper-

94

ors before them, a number of Silla kings believed themselves to be a Buddha. This type of reasoning was probably possible because the historical Buddha was also descended from a royal bloodline. It would have been easy for the kings of Silla to feel that they had something in common with Buddha. If a king is a Buddha, nobles and commoners alike had to submit to him unconditionally because there is no other being on earth whose authority exceeded that of the Buddha. In addition, this principle would have been the perfect strategy for strengthening the throne. This is the political motive that lay behind the religious slogan that 'Silla is the Buddha land'.

However, no amount of slogan-wielding could have won support without evidence to back up the words. Because this world is based on materiality, people need to be shown something that is visible and tangible. This is why construction on Bulguksa was begun. In other words, Bulguksa is a miniature version of a Buddha Land specifically created for all to see. It was meant to be a memorial-esque sign that proved the sacred equation 'Silla = land of the Buddha'. This would then make the king of Silla as well as its people the chosen people of Buddhism; the Silla government attempted to reflect this fact as well in the construction of Bulguksa.

Why was it called Bulguksa?: The Structure   After naming the temple Bulguksa, the Silla government designed it to befit its name.

To achieve this effect, the Silla government decided to enshrine all of the most important Buddhas in this temple to really make Bulguksa the Buddha Land. Which Buddha is the most important one in Buddhism? As mentioned earlier, there are countless Buddhas within the boundaries of Buddhist doctrine. Why so many Buddhas? Of course, the only Buddha who actually existed was the Śākyamuni Buddha who lived and died(approximately) 2500 years ago in India. The word 'Śākyamuni' is a common noun that means a 'holy one^muni' who is from the Sakya tribe.[b) The word 'Buddha' is also a common noun which means 'the awakened one', indicating an enlightened person. But there are many types of Buddhas who appear in Buddhist scriptures.

For example, Amitabha Buddha waits in paradise for sentient beings to arrive and Medicine Buddha^Sansk. Bhaisajyaguru holds up a medicine bottle to cure the illnesses of sentient beings. There is also Vairocana Buddha, the Sanskrit name for Dharma Body Buddha. There is a different story behind the origins of each of these various Buddhas. For example, Vairocana Buddha came into being in order to explain the success of Śākyamuni Buddha as Buddhist doctrine developed. This Buddha will be explained further shortly. There are also Buddhas who were created to accommodate the prayers of the common people; Amitabha Buddha is a representative example because he was created as the guardian of paradise, the place that all

Buddhists hope to enter after they die. These two Buddhas eventually came to be considered second in importance only to Śākyamuni Buddha. As a result, many temples formed that worshipped these three Buddhas — Śākyamuni, Vairocana and Amitabha.

Why were these three Buddhas considered so important? There is no need to explain the case of Śākyamuni Buddha: he is an actual historic figure based on which the massive religious tradition known as Buddhism was established. As the founder of Buddhism, being treated with respect is an obvious consequence. On the other hand, Amitabha Buddha is the Buddha in charge of paradise, which is the Buddhist version of heaven. According to Buddhist doctrine, anyone who repeats the oath 'I take refuge in Amitabha Buddha' just ten times or even just once will automatically be guided to paradise at the moment of death. As such, doctrines that have to do with the Amitabha Buddha are not difficult to understand at all. This also explains why Amitabha Buddha is so popular with Buddhist lay believers. By following exactly the Buddhist doctrines as they have been set up, people can rely on Śākyamuni Buddha in life and enjoy eternal bliss in paradise governed by Amitabha Buddha after death. As such, these two Buddhas are in charge of the life and afterlife of Buddhist believers; if you take a look at Bulguksa you can see that the *beopdang* that houses these Buddhas is divided into two parts. As shown in the blueprint of Bulguksa, the section that houses these two most important Buddhas is in the front center of the building. There is an auditorium-like space behind Main Hall where Śākyamuni Buddha is housed. This is a public space where monks gather to study or have meetings.

Behind the Main Hall area are Vairocana Buddha Hall^{Kor.} ^{Birojeon} and Avalokiteśvara Shrine^{Kor. Gwaneumjeon}. The first to appear is Vairocana Buddha Hall, which of course houses Vairocana Buddha. But as this Buddha is not very easy to understand, here is a very rough overview. After having only worshipped the historical Buddha, Buddhists began to have doubts as time passed. They began to question what force was behind or the cause of the existence of the historic Śākyamuni Buddha. Believers thus invented a being as an answer to this question and that being was named Vairocana Buddha. This Buddha is sometimes also translated as the Buddha of Law or the Buddha of Truth; these names indicate that this Buddha is the embodiment of Buddhist truth. We can then conclude that this Buddha is absolute and that he exists only conceptually as a being who has risen above this world. This explanation may seem a little obtuse, but it is actually the same for Christianity. Jesus, like Buddha, was an actual historical figure but the source or origin of his existence on earth was God. In a similar web of relationships, Vairocana Buddha plays the same role as God. But because Vairocana Buddha was a largely theoretical concept it was not very popular with lay believers. Perhaps it is due to this fact that the area of Vairocana Buddha is smaller than that of Śākyamuni or Amitabha Buddha.

Right next to the domain of Vairocana Buddha is Avalok-itesvara Shrine, which houses Guanyin. As stated earlier, Bulguk-sa houses the most important Buddhas and the Guanyin inside Avalokiteśvara Shrine is the only bodhisattva of the group. This shows that Guanyin was the most popular bodhisattva with lay be-lievers. The most important function of religion is above all the abili-ty to pray to another being to receive luck. Guanyin is the best suited for this role within Buddhism. According to Buddhist scripture, she is an entity with 1000 eyes and 1000 hands who rushes over im-mediately to aid a person in distress. Guanyin became increasingly popular and eventually came to occupy her own area within Bulguk-sa. This is how Bulguksa became the Buddha Land. The three most important Buddhas and their secretary Guanyin together form a sort of Buddha Land dream team. Leaving the background explanation at this, let's now go inside the temple.

At the Front Courtyard of Bulguksa

The Path to Bulguksa   There is a large parking lot in front of Bulguksa. There is also a large gate called the 'one-pillared gate'. The one-pillared gate of most Korean temples is the gate at the entrance. Already we can see a deviation from the original appearance of the temple. Even a national temple could not have had such a large plaza in the front. This type of wide open plaza is not a familiar space to Koreans. The same goes for this one-pillared gate: at the time that this temple was built during the Silla dynasty, a one-pillared gate was not built. Some say that this gate was created

• • The Path to Bulguksa

during the Joseon dynasty. Let's head toward Bulguksa with these thoughts in mind. The first thing you will see is the Bridge of Great Freedom. Once you cross it, there will be a Four Deva Gate like the one at Seokguram Grotto. Crossing another bridge will bring you to the front courtyard of Bulguksa.

It is impossible to know what this path really looked like because this path, the second bridge and the gate were all constructed in modern times. But one thing that is certain is that these would not have been so smooth-surfaced if they were built long ago. I also have doubts about whether there would have been several ponds and two bridges along this short path. I think that modern Koreans who did not think very highly of artifact preservation did not do a proper job here. You will notice that the path is slightly curved: this is a traditional Korean method. Koreans usually do not build paths leading to building entrances in straight lines.

We have confirmed this fact with Changdeok Palace and Jongmyo in Seoul. If you go to Changdeok Palace or Jongmyo, you will see that the Main Hall of both buildings cannot be seen from the main entrance gate. This is because the main gate and Main Hall are not built along the same axis. Koreans have a tendency of revealing the most important building gradually in stages. In other words, Koreans prefer to not have the main character emerge at once but for it to gradually reveal itself to show everything only at the end of the path. Bulguksa has used this same method in creating the path to its main building. There is no point along this path at which the entire main building comes into sight at once. Creating the road like this from the entrance point is a technique that is rarely found in neighboring countries like China or Japan.

An Imperfect Restoration: The disappearance of the pond

When looking directly at the front of Bulguksa, it is difficult to see the entire view because there are many trees. Perhaps this is why advertising posters of Bulguksa always show the side view. However, this is a grave error because Bulguksa was originally built to be viewed from the front. The reason for this will be explained shortly. As stated earlier, Bulguksa is the embodiment of Buddha Land. We must not forget that all of the architectural devices of this temple are there to prove that the area within the temple is the Buddha Land. Our guide will also be based on this premise.

Before going into an explanation of this temple's architecture, I would like to point out that the front part of this temple has not been restored properly. Not having restored this properly is a grave error because the things installed in the front section were very important architectural features of this temple when it was first being constructed. The pond that was in the front is the most important of these. The grass that now covers this spot makes the possibility of a pond seem unlikely, but there definitely used to be a pond here. We know this because a pond foundation $^{40m \times 25.5m, \; 131' \times 66'}$ was discovered here in a 1969 excavation on this site.

The significance of this pond is explained in various ways by Buddhist doctrine. One theory argues that this pond symbolizes the suffering-filled world between this world and the next world while another states that it is a pond in paradise. If the first theory is correct, where we are standing would be this world while the area inside the temple would be Buddha Land. One Buddhist scripture states that ordinary people like us must cross over water and travel over the clouds to reach Buddha Land; this is embodied by Bulguksa. To achieve this effect, a pond was created as well as the Blue Cloud Bridge$^{Cheong \; un \; Gyo}$ and White Cloud Bridge$^{Baek \; un \; Gyo}$. The steps leading to the temple represent these cloud bridges. After having climbed the steps, Golden Purple Gate^{Jahamun} appears. Why purple? In China purple was considered the best color because it was the color of the emperor. Because of this, the Chinese believed that Buddha's body radiated purple light like the emperor. You can see the Buddha once you enter this door. But let's go inside to see the Buddha a little later and redirect our focus to the front of the temple.

This pond was oval-shaped and was fairly large, having measured 40 meters$^{approx. \; 131ft}$ in diameter. A pictorial representation would look as below. Evidence that proves that a pond was here still

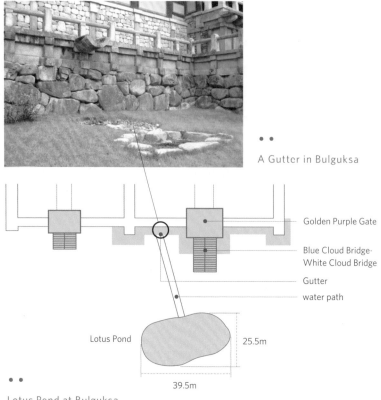

A Gutter in Bulguksa

Golden Purple Gate

Blue Cloud Bridge·
White Cloud Bridge

Gutter

water path

Lotus Pond

25.5m

39.5m

Lotus Pond at Bulguksa

exists today. As can be seen in the photograph, a gutter was installed at the foundation stones so that water could flow out. It is said that a rainbow would rise with a spray of water when water flowed to the pond from the gutter, making a beautiful sight. All of this proves that the pond did exist, but the real question is why it was made in the first place. The reason for this was mentioned briefly earlier in relation to Buddhist doctrines. I believe that the pond would also have had an architectural function as well as a symbolic one.

A pond in this spot would reflect the beautiful façade of Bulguksa. The appearance that is reflected here would have been no ordinary sight. This will be mentioned again later but a great deal of care was invested in decorating the front part of Bulguksa. For example, even the steps leading up to the temple are extraordinary. This stairway not only fulfills its function as a stairway but is itself an outstanding architectural work. Thus, this stairway is an independent architectural masterpiece apart from its relationship to this temple. There are also two beautiful pavilions in front of Bulguksa, and of these the one in the center is particularly breathtaking. This pavilion is outlined even more clearly because it protrudes outward, and the pond would have been located below. In this case, the beautiful stairway, stone wall and pavilion would be reflected on the pond's surface. This reflection would have been provided for the enjoyment of visitors to the temple. A worshipper would see the grand façade of the temple as he gradually approached closer, and would have mentally prepared himself while looking up this sight. This alone would have no doubt been a magnificent view. But it was provided a second time through the reflection of the pond. Wouldn't this combined sight have brought a sense of rapture to the worshipper?

In order to get a clear sense of all this, you need to view Bulguksa front and center. But large pine trees that have been planted in front of the temple prevent a full view of this formerly beautiful front section. Most religious structures are built in a grand and dignified style so as to inspire a feeling of pious devotion in the worshipper. Bulguksa is a dignified structure that has the widest front section of all Korean temples. It overwhelms the viewer. We who come to visit Bulguksa should also be awed and overwhelmed, but there is no need to worry about that because of the randomly planted large trees. This is why it is such a colossal error. Of course, the fact that the absence of the pond prevents a view of its reflection goes without saying. Both the pond's reflection as well as the façade itself would have been beautiful, but none of this can be seen today. Every time I visit Bulguksa, I cannot avoid feeling that I was cheated into paying the admission fee because I am prevented from viewing the temple as it should be viewed.

The Stately Appearance of Buddha Land   Let us leave behind our discussion of the pond and go through each feature of the façade one by one. Seen from the front, it is divided into two areas and each area has a main gate. Looking at the building, I have already mentioned that the right is Buddha Land and the left is the land of Amitabha Buddha. Because this is the world of the Buddhas, this space should be sacred and clearly distinguished from this world below. This effect can be achieved by raising the building high off the ground. Religious buildings are often built tall, but there is a reason for all this. Bulguksa achieved this effect by stacking stones to create a platform. To achieve an even more dignified look, two platforms were stacked. But there is something interesting about the composition of these platforms. As you can see in the photograph, the bottom platform was created with natural stones while the top platform was made by stacking stones that had been formatted by hand. It may have been an attempt to create a harmony between nature and artificial craftsmanship. But a highly

• •

Two Platforms of Bulguksa

• •

The 'Grangie' Method Shown in the Bottom Platform

interesting point was discovered in the bottom platform. A close-up of the bottom platforms shows that the natural stones were stacked without a second thought and the top platform was placed on top; the juncture of these two deserves some attention. The natural stones were not adjusted to fit the artificially carved stones but vice versa. This technique is known as the 'Grangie' method.

This method is rarely found in China or Japan and is unique to Korea. Firstly, it is an advanced technique from an engineering perspective. Positioning the stones in this way is said to be effective against any earthquake. There is also an aesthetic aspect. Traditional Koreans tried to add as little human touch to architecture and landscaping as possible. This stylistic tendency is expressed in the use of natural uncut stones in the platform, but this is taken one step further by adjusting the stones to make them look more natural. The attempt by Koreans to become closer to nature is evident not only in antiquity as in Silla but continues right up to the Joseon dynasty as well. More detailed information on this topic can be found by referring to my other book, *Understanding Koreans and Their Culture*. It is unfortunate that this mindset is not evident in modern Koreans. Koreans lost contact with their past traditions during Japanese colonial rule, and seem to have lost that profound sense due to their successive fascination with Western culture. But it is unlikely that this sense has been lost for good; it will probably become gradually revived in the future.

As we have seen thus far, the defining characteristic of the façade of Bulguksa is the tall stacked platform. There is almost no other temple in Korea that has been built in this way. It was meant to express the magnificence of the Buddha Land. But upon close inspection, the area of Śākyamuni as seen from the front center is raised higher and wider than that of Amitabha Buddha. Not only is the foundation one increment higher but it is also protrudes outward. This is because Śākyamuni is the Buddha who is in charge of this world. Because he built temples here in this world, the Buddha who is connected to this world is considered more important. The steps that are in front of Śākyamuni's domain are much bigger and steeper than those in front of Amitabha Buddha's domain. The steps in front of the domain of the former are probably the most magnificent looking steps among all Korean temples. Perhaps this is why these steps are not considered merely an accessory but is recognized for its own value as a beautiful work of art. The value of the steps is able to stand alone. To get an idea of how much care and attention was invested in building them, a look at the side view is sufficient. It is not clearly visible in the photograph, but we can see that the stones in the center were formed into a sort of double trapezoid by the arch-like structure at the top. Building a double layer like this is able to hold whether pressure is applied from above or below. Typically the stones are made to interlock with each other in only one section; there used to be no such cases in which the stones both above and below were fitted together like this one. It is even able to withstand an earthquake without much difficulty. Even if pressure is applied

• •

The Side View of the Blue Cloud Bridge

from many directions as in an earthquake, the structure will not collapse. The fact that such sophisticated techniques were applied to
even minor details is definite proof that this temple was indeed a
royal temple. Most nobles would not have been able to hire construction work done to this degree of perfection and thoroughness.

One of the cliché explanations that is always mentioned
when explaining these steps is that there are 33 steps in total. The
number of steps has to do with Buddhist doctrine; to briefly summarize for our purposes, there are 33 worlds that we must cross to
reach the realm of Buddha from this world. These worlds are said to

GYEONGJU, The Heart of Korean Culture

be stacked perpendicularly and the world of Buddha is at the very top. I am not quite sure what this is supposed to mean. If Buddha's world is at the very top, countless questions may arise ranging from 'how do you know that there is no other world above that' to 'is there an end to this at all'. This is why some argue that 33 worlds are not actual worlds outside but related to the condition of the mind. In any case, opening the Golden Purple Gate after having climbed the 33 steps leads right to Śākyamuni Buddha.

Having seen these steps, let us also take a look at those in front of Amitabha Buddha's area as well. As you can see, these steps are much simpler than those for Śākyamuni. It is unavoidable because the stone platform is not very high. One notable feature is that each step has a depressed engraving of a lotus flower on it. The name of this 'bridge' most likely originates from 'lotus flower and the seven jewels'. It is meant to be a faithful interpretation of a section of Buddhist scripture, according to which paradise is decorated with

● ●

The Shape of Lotus Flower engraved on the Bridge

seven jewels and to reach it one must travel on a lotus flower. But this design must be viewed from above. We will come back to this once inside the temple; people used to be able to walk freely up and down the steps, but now there are so many tourists that entrance is restricted. It is a cruel twist of irony that I could freely use these steps when I did not know anything about this temple but now that I do I cannot use them at will.

Another aspect of the façade of this temple that deserves our attention is the two pavilions found at each end. Of the two the pavilion on the left catches the eye because it is elaborately designed. The one on the right is very simple in comparison. The reason for such a large degree of contrast between the two styles probably has something to do with Seokgatap and Dabotap in the inner courtyard of the temple. The ornate pavilion is located on the side of the simply designed Seokgatap and the undecorated pavilion is in front of Dabotap, the splendor of which is rarely found in any other Korean pagoda. This layout is meant to achieve a balance; it is easier to understand when looking at the blueprint. If you connect the Buddha statue in *beopdang* on the blueprint and Seokgatap, it connects to the fancy pavilion on the left; connecting the Buddha statue to Dabotap leads to the simple pavilion on the right. This is most likely the design of the architect of this temple. The defining characteristic of these pavilions is found in the layout of the first floor. The

112

Gyeonghueru at
Gyeongbok Palace in Seoul

second floor was built in the structure of a house but the first floor, albeit built from stone, was built in imitation of wooden architecture. When building a pavilion, the first floor is typically designed as a pillar. For example, let us envision Gyeonghueru at Gyeongbok Palace, the largest pavilion. The upper floor is quite decorated, but the bottom floor simply consists of stone pillars.

But it is obvious that a great deal of care was taken on the bottom floors of the pavilions at Bulguksa. They could have been built as pillars but instead they have been highly decorated. The pavilion on the left is particularly evident. Let's get an overall picture of this pavilion. The bottom platform was stacked with natural stones on top of which the pillar of the pavilion was placed, but a careful inspection reveals that it is not a pillar. It is a simplified version of what would be the bottom part of the eaves of a wooden

Two Pavilions in the front part of Bulguksa: Beomyeongnu and Gyeongnu

building. The stone was crafted with a high degree of skill. It is the work of Silla master artisans who believed that none could challenge their skill in carving granite. It creates a clear contrast with the natural uncarved stones that make up the bottom layer. This can also be interpreted as an architectural device. To show that Buddha Land is located in the far reaches of the sky that exceeds all earthly imagination, eaves were crafted out of stone and the pavilion was built on top of it. In other words, the Buddha Land is an extremely exalted place that rests above the roof. Also, because the stones are crafted in the style of wooden buildings, it matches nicely with the actual wooden structure that rests on top of it. It is because of such exacting craftsmanship that it took 30 years to build.

This wraps up everything that needs to be said about the façade of Bulguksa. The reason why there is so much to say about the front of the temple is that so much care was devoted to the work. It is an unavoidable consequence in that because a temple is where Buddha resides, the degree of decoration could be no less than magnificent. The highlight of this temple is the façade and the two pagodas in the inner courtyard. Before we see these, there is one more thing to see: the corridor encircling the entire temple. This type of corridor is usually meant to be inside the palace. But as with almost all heritage items in Korea, Bulguksa was also burned to the ground during the Hideyoshi Invasion in the late sixteenth century.[7] The most important buildings were rebuilt soon afterwards but these corridors only managed to be renovated in the early 1970s. Perhaps this is why there is something awkward about this corridor. It looks rather stuffy and oppressive. It is incomprehensible how people who crafted the foundation stones and the two pagodas of this temple could stand to create something as low-quality as this corridor. Nothing about this corridor reminds me of Silla. But fixing it is not really possible as there is no way of knowing what the original corridor looked like. Renovation technology in relation to cultural heritage items in Korea in the 1970s was sub-par. Compared to now, the difference is like night and day. I remember what Bulguksa looked like without the corridor because I visited many times before it was rebuilt and am forced to conclude that the temple looked better without the corridor. It is pretty clear that this corridor was renovated incorrectly. I sometimes get the thought that the color scheme is strange but cannot move beyond discontent because there is no real alternative. Leaving all these complaints aside, let's now at last enter the temple.

Inside Bulguksa

Inside Bulguksa 1: In front of the two best pagodas in Korea

To enter the temple you must enter through the right corridor. Of course, this is not the proper entrance. There is no reason that people would have entered on the side while leaving alone the front entrance. Furthermore, this temple would have only been used by the royal family and high-ranking nobles because it was funded by the palace; such visitors would not have used the side entrance. It is most likely the case today because there are so many tourists who visit every day. In any case, once you have entered the front courtyard through that entrance your path will be blocked by two pagodas. These two pagodas, Seokgatap and Dabotap, are recognized as the best pagodas in all Korean history. Both of them having been designated as National Treasures, their quality needs no further qualification. As with the façade of Bulguksa, there is a great deal to cover concerning these pagodas. Before we begin, I think now would be a good time for a brief explanation about pagodas for readers who are not familiar with Buddhism.

In Buddhism, a pagoda is basically the grave of Buddha. Buddha instructed on many occasions not to build his statue after his death. However, his disciples wished to pay their respects to their teacher and this eventually came to be embodied in the form of a pagoda. The pagoda was known as Buddha's grave because it is where the remains of his cremation were stored. The history of the development of the pagoda is extremely long and complicated; it is not only impossible to cover in its entirety but there is also no need to go this far. But for a very brief overview, there was no *beopdang* in early temples for the Buddha statue and only a pagoda. Because of this, the pagoda was extremely large. But as the Buddha statue came into being around the start of the Common Era, the focus of worship gradually shifted away from the pagoda to the Buddha statue inside *beopdang*. Consequently the pagoda became smaller while the *beopdang* became larger and more grandiose. Bulguksa was constructed in the midst of this phenomenon. However, this does not mean that the pagoda became tiny. Based on the size of the inner courtyard, Seokgatap and Dabotap are quite large, making the courtyard feel slightly cramped. I get the feeling that reconstruction on these was also not a perfect process but do not yet know exactly what went wrong(this probably has to do with the fact that the corridor was not rebuilt correctly).

With these thoughts in mind, it is easy to see that these two pagodas look very different from each other. Not only are they different but the two respective styles are at opposite ends of the spectrum. One[Seokgatap] is the epitome of simplicity while the other one[Dabotap] is the height of opulence. When I visit here on a field trip

Seokgatap(left) and Dabotap(right)

with my students they usually gravitate toward Dabotap. To a novice Dabotap seems a lot more elegant. On the other hand, Seokgatap does not seem to have any distinguishing features. It is plain to the point of being insipid. This is why Seokgatap is not popular with beginners. There is no way of knowing why it was chosen to be a National Treasure. However, once you understand that Seokgatap is much more difficult to construct than Dabotap, Dabotap looks like a mere supplementary attachment of Seokgatap(this is not to say that Dabotap is not beautiful). However, it is not easy to be at the level at which you can recognize this difference.

The explanation of cultural tour guides about these pagodas is always the same. The explanation usually goes something like the following while citing Lotus Sutra, a Buddhist scripture: There was once a Buddha named Dabo — as I have mentioned earlier, there are many Buddhas in Buddhism! — who declared to his disciples that he would honor with a pagoda encrusted in jewels anyone who could give a sermon on the Lotus Sutra. A compressed version of the rest of the story is that eventually Śākyamuni gave a sermon on this sutra and at that moment Dabotap rose up out of the ground. The location of these two pagodas in the front courtyard of this temple is said to be an earthly representation of the above story. However, this explanation does not help us appreciate the beauty of these pagodas.

There are many stories in Mahayana scriptures that defy

logical understanding. It is thus easy to lose one's way by relying solely on the scriptures. Let us then extract only the essence of what this story is trying to say before moving on. This story was created to show that Śākyamuni was indeed a truly enlightened individual. Buddhist monks invented many stories to prove that their teacher was awakened to the truth of life and the universe; this is one of them. They created a fictional Buddha, Dabo Buddha, and had him confess that Śākyamuni was the true awakened one. This attempt is not only found in Buddhism. The same occurs in Christianity. In Christianity, what kind of person was John the Baptist shown to be? Regardless of the fact that he was a prophet in his own right — some say that John was more popular than Jesus in his day — we cannot avoid receiving the impression that he was simply 'used' to prove that Jesus was the son of God. If we apply this framework to Buddhism, Dabotap is John while Seokgatap is Jesus. This will suffice for discussion on complex religious theory.

Research indicates that Dabotap imitates the format of a pagoda that was highly popular in the Sarnath region near Varanashi, India. This format was brought into Silla through the Silk Road via Central Asia and China, but it never became popular in Silla. We can know this because there is no subsequent pagoda that was built in the same ornate style. As shown in the photograph, rectangles, octagons and circle shapes were stacked together to form a very romantic and

• •
A Pagoda at Sarnath near Varanashi
©Bongryul Kim

fancy design. This may have been an attempt to express the soul by overlapping the circle, the perfect shape, with octagons and rectangular shapes. The fact that sturdy granite was crafted into such unbelievably soft and flowing form should also be kept in mind. It is easy to mistakenly think that this pagoda was constructed out of wood. It is to this extent that even the small details are well-crafted. Architects say that Dabotap is a wooden structure that was converted into a stone one. But sources show that construction work on this pagoda was finished earlier than for Seokgatap. At a glance, it seems that the plain Seokgatap would be easier to create, but Silla artisans finished Dabotap first. How did this happen?

It is easy for those who are not accustomed to the arts to think that between Seokgatap and Dabotap, it is much more difficult to construct the latter. It is because Dabotap is extremely fancy. However, those who are familiar with art all agree that Seokgatap is the more difficult piece to create. The reason for this is simple. There is nothing to add or detract from Seokgatap. It achieved success with just a few simple stones. This is not because Silla architects did not know how to use sophisticated and fancy techniques but because the Silla sense of design was on such an advanced level. It is said that the most difficult design is one that represents the most with the least. Beginners keep adding superfluous parts because they can not do this. Experts are able to confidently cut out everything that is unnecessary and leave only the most basic form. Every time I look at Seokgatap I can sense that it was a true professional who created Seokgatap. Only a few stones were used without any other decorations

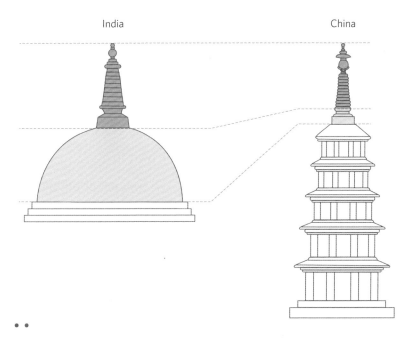

India   China

Comparison of Pagodas of India and China

to create the perfect balance of proportions. Because this pagoda was created with perfect proportion, nothing created by subsequent master artisans has exceeded it. This is why Seokgatap is considered to have the best form among Korean pagodas.

We can go into an entire new discussion on the history of development of the Korean pagoda, but this is merely a burden to those who are not familiar with Buddhist culture. Even if it is covered here, it is soon forgotten. For cases like this it is best to simply deliver the key point. With this objective, let's go over the history of Korean pagodas. The format of the pagoda of course came from China; in short, it is a Chinese-style house. When the pagoda came into China after having crossed Central Asia from India, while the Chinese did not completely overlook the Indian format they did fix it to a large degree to create their own format. The Chinese, believing that the pagoda was the home of Buddha, began to construct pagodas that looked very much like their own houses. To achieve this effect the Chinese went through various trial and error attempts with a variety of materials like wood or brick, but the material that they liked best was brick. The Chinese used their own brick houses as the model for the pagoda. All of these traditions were then sent on to Silla, where the people of Silla after numerous attempts decided on not brick but stone. The climax of these attempts resulted in Seokgatap. Of course, Seokgatap was not created at once but required

a testing process of 100 years to become what we see today.

To integrate what we have just covered, a pagoda is basically a house made of stone. This is why traces of wooden architecture can be clearly seen. For example, the foundation stones as well as the four corners of each floor bear traces of the pillars that are used when building a house. Also, each floor is covered by a roof: this can be seen as the eaves. Wooden buildings have eaves between the pillar and roof; this can be seen as a simplified version of this. In any case, Seokgatap is the epitome of simplicity. Korean art has various characteristics; one of them is the tendency to express or recreate an object in simplified terms. It ignores the inner details and makes a large and simplified expression. Seokgatap is a model example of this type of naiveté. As stated earlier, no subsequent pagoda has been able to surpass Seokgatap. This is because it is impossible to be simpler than Seokgatap. All the pagodas created afterwards in cities throughout Korea have merely slightly altered the format or added some decoration, but none has been able to develop the original form of Seokgatap any further(i.e. decorating the foundation stones with statues of gods who come out in Buddhist scriptures).

This covers almost everything about these two pagodas, but we still have not seen the most important feature. This point is largely unknown outside a handful of professionals. But we must not forget that this is one of the important qualities that make Bulguksa a World Cultural Heritage. The most important point in appreciating the two pagodas is that two polar opposite structures that were built for separate purposes are placed in the same location. To explain this in a different way for easier understanding, as I have stated many times Seokgatap is the epitome of simplicity while Dabotap is the epitome of opulence. Thus, Seokgatap and Dabotap can be said to each express 'masculine power and feminine softness', 'regulation and idiosyncrasy', 'practical and theoretical', 'traditional and romantic'. It was the intention of the person who built Bulguksa to integrate two opposing ideas by placing two diametrically opposite structures in one space.

It is easy for two structures as entirely different from one another as Seokgatap and Dabotap to push each other out if placed in the same space because they are so different. They are unable to accept each other because the difference is too extreme. However, this does not happen in this space. This is because Seokgatap and Dabotap complement each other very well. It is a result of the person who placed them here who predicted this and designed it in this way, but this type of positioning would have been an impossible task without a great deal of confidence. In other words, this design could only have been executed by an expert among experts. The easiest design is repetition of the same thing. This results in a run-of-the-mill design that neither stands out nor is unreasonable.

This type of safe and moderate design of space actually began to be used for temples constructed after Bulguksa. Most Korean temples have two pagodas similar to Seokgatap in front of their Main Hall. It is the safest way to position them. An attempt to bring out the aesthetics of Seokgatap and Dabotap without any sense of beauty would have resulted in a strange looking work of art. In fact, a person without such sense would not have even thought of placing these two together from the first place. This shows just how advanced the artistic level of Silla was at the time that this temple was constructed. Then again, a country that could create an absolute masterpiece like Seokguram Grotto was able to have such an experimental work right on the front courtyard of Bulguksa.

However, this dualistic concept of beauty is not found only

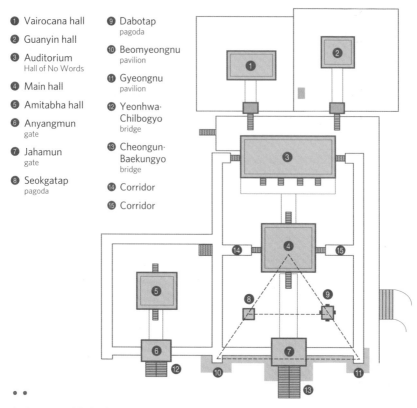

① Vairocana hall
② Guanyin hall
③ Auditorium
   Hall of No Words
④ Main hall
⑤ Amitabha hall
⑥ Anyangmun
   gate
⑦ Jahamun
   gate
⑧ Seokgatap
   pagoda
⑨ Dabotap
   pagoda
⑩ Beomyeongnu
   pavilion
⑪ Gyeongnu
   pavilion
⑫ Yeonhwa·
   Chilbogyo
   bridge
⑬ Cheongun·
   Baekungyo
   bridge
⑭ Corridor
⑮ Corridor

A site map of Bulguksa

in these two pagodas. We saw two pavilions in front of the temple before entering. These pavilions look rather different from one another. Compared to the fancy one on the left facing Bulguksa, the pavilion on the right is very plain. Why is there such a contrast? The standard explanation is that this is related to the two pavilions in the front courtyard. In other words, the plain and humble-looking pavilion was placed in front of the fancy Dabotap and the ornate pavilion was placed in front of the simple Seokgatap. In this way, an artistic balance was created. Here we can see the meticulous care of the architect in taking care of even the most minor details. However, this type of construction does not end here. As shown in the photograph below, there is another order. This occurs by drawing a line between the two pavilions and the two pagodas and connecting them to the Buddha statue in Main Hall. A triangular structure is thus formed and this is what gives stability to the overall structure and layout of the front courtyard. We must realize that the front courtyard, the highlight of Bulguksa, was created through such precise geometric calculations.

This covers all of the important points about the two pagodas, but there are still minute details that have not been seen. First, observe the surrounding area of the bottom section of Seokgatap. We can see that eight stones in the shape of lotus flowers have been placed along the edges. Forgoing all complicated explanation, it is enough to envision Buddha's supporters praising Buddha while sitting on these lotus flowers. The lotus flowers are their positions. What attracts our attention even more than these are the rough stones that are located right next to the pagoda in uninterrupted succession. As can be seen in the photograph, some untrimmed stones are spread over the ground for no apparent reason: what could have happened?

• •

The surrounding area of the Bottom Section of Seokgatap

People who were capable of creating Seokgatap could not have placed these rough stones here for no reason. We should assume that it was a highly calculated move. Had these stones been here from the beginning, they could have easily been cleared away so that the pagoda could rest on smooth ground. But this did obviously did not happen. What could have been the purpose of this?

First of all, there seems to be a conceptual aspect. According-ing to legend, when Buddha attained enlightenment under a Bodhi tree he was meditating while sitting atop a rock. Thus, if Seokgatap symbolizes Buddha as I have stated earlier, then the stones at the base of the pagoda could represent the rock that Buddha was sitting on. Can there be another explanation for this? This may be a shot in the dark, but I think that the answer may have to do with the unconventional aesthetic sense of Koreans in placing such rough stones right beside a highly structured pagoda like Seokgatap. An observation of Korean art regardless of era reveals a rejection of orderliness. I think that Koreans have an innate tendency of disliking perfection.

For example, there is the dislike of perfect symmetry. This does not mean that Koreans cannot or do not create perfectly symmetrical things. However there are many instances in which after creating a perfect object something is done to break apart that perfection. Examples of this can be seen in the grangie technique used on the platforms of Bulguksa and the different designs of the pavilions on the right and left sides of the entrance to the temple. Both of these examples are unconventional expressions. Thus I wonder whether Seokgatap is in the same category as these. As stated earlier, Seokgatap was geometrically calculated to be perfectly symmetrical. However, it seems that the people of Silla did not like such stifling perfection. While they could not touch Seokgatap itself, they instead decided to adjust the surroundings by spreading around some uncut stones. In this way, they alleviated the tension that results from having perfect order. However, as the Korean saying goes, my theory could be the 'explanation that exceeds the quality of the dream':

there is a high probability that all of this is teleological and thus should be approached with caution.

We should now turn to the rest of the temple, but there is one more point to mention about Seokgatap before we leave the pagodas behind. This is that the oldest printed book in the world was found inside it. Called the Dharani Sutra, dharani is an incantation used in Buddhism and the book in which this incantation was written out was found inside Seokgatap. With a width of only 6.6 centimeters[approx. 2.6in] it is a tiny book, but it is also in scroll form and is 6 meters[approx. 19.7ft] long. Because Seokgatap was completed in 751, it is assumed that this book was printed before then; if this is true, this book becomes the oldest book in the world. However, there are a few unsolved problems surrounding this book and thus it has not been registered as a Memory of the World by UNESCO. If this book really is the oldest printed book in the world, it should without question be registered but this has not been done. Why has this happened? First of all, there

The Dharani Sutra found inside Seokgatap

is a theory that this book was not printed in Korea but was actually printed in China and imported by Korea. As a theory argued by the Chinese, Korean academics of course refuse to accept it. In any case, the debate has not fully been resolved. Also, another theory is that this book was not placed inside Seokgatap when the latter was constructed but could have been placed inside in the eleventh century when Seokgatap was undergoing renovations. In general, this book is still at the center of raging controversy, but Korean academia continues to insist that this book is the oldest printed book in the world.

Inside Bulguksa 2: A round of the buildings Having seen these two pagodas is the equivalent of having seen almost all of Bulguksa. The façade and pagodas are that important. From here onward, we can skim through the rest of the temple before we leave. Let's first look at the buildings. The majority of the buildings we see inside the temple were rebuilt in the 1970s. The only buildings that are older that that are Main Hall and Golden Purple Gate, the gate to the Main Hall area, behind the two pagodas and the Hall of Supreme Bliss. However, even this Hall of Supreme Bliss was not built during the Silla dynasty. Apart from a very small minority, all old buildings in Korea were burned to the ground when Japan invaded in the late sixteenth century; thus, Bulguksa is no exception. Even after the war had ended, lack of funds prevented reconstruction work from begin-

● ● The Side View of the Steps in front of the Bulguksa

ning right away. The buildings that we have seen so far were rebuilt as late as the mid-eighteenth century. However, one point to keep in mind about Bulguksa architecture is that the buildings date back to Joseon but the foundational platforms are originally from Silla, more specifically the mid-eighth century. Thus, an inspection of the platforms reveals the high quality of Silla design. The best way to feel this is through the steps in front of the temple. This is a point that tourists often miss entirely, but as can be seen in the photograph the side view of the steps shows that they were constructed with a very fluid outline. This is the Silla idea of beauty. The transformation of hard granite into such flowing lines could only have been accomplished by someone with an outstanding sense of aesthetics. No detail was too small to overlook in decorating this temple. It was the same degree of skill that made possible the creation of such beautiful outlines that also created the two pagodas in the front courtyard.

In sharp contrast to these beautiful lines, I cannot avoid feeling that renovations done by subsequent generations look clumsily done. First of all, the structures of the foundations and the buildings do not match very well because the foundations were built in the Silla dynasty while the buildings were built according to Joseon architectural style. There is a difference of approximately 1000 years. However, this does not usually catch the eye of ordinary visitors because it is a technical point that would only be recognizable to professionals. I myself also learned this from a book written by an expert in the field. As I have stated previously, the corridors that block each domain also look rather strange, especially the connecting parts. The thought vaguely comes to mind that a Silla architect with a good aesthetic sense would not have constructed it in this way, but there is no way of knowing the original form. Even my colleague who is a Korean architecture major has no answer to this question, so there is no way for us non-specialists to know either.

Although the buildings do have their limitations, it is impossible not to take a look inside Main Hall after having come all this way. If you look inside Main Hall you will see three Buddha statues. Of course, the center statue is Śākyamuni and the ones on either side of him are his assistant bodhisattvas. Buddha statues are often arranged in sets of three, but the rules to such arrangement are complex. Only certain bodhisattvas can be placed next to Śākyamuni if the latter is in the middle but it is not necessary for ordinary readers to know all of these details. In addition, there is no need to pay much attention to the statues housed in Main Hall because they are not that old. After a brief look at Main Hall, let's go to the building right behind it. This is an auditorium where the monks who live here study and hold meetings. As this building was also rebuilt 40 years ago, there is no need to stay here for long either. However, the name of this building is eye-catching. The name is 'Museoljeon', which translates in English into 'Hall of No Words'. This is related to one of the doctrines espoused by Buddhism. Buddhism and Zen Buddhism in particular argue that ultimate truth cannot be verbally expressed. According to Korean Buddhists, Buddha said toward the end of his life that 'I have not said a single word'; this building was probably named after this episode.

As mentioned earlier, behind this domain are the domain of Vairocana Buddha, considered a god in Buddhism, and that of Guanyin, the most popular bodhisattva. We have already discussed

Vairocana Buddha in a previous section but the Buddha statue housed here is also designated as a National Treasure. The classification of 'National Treasure' is a huge honor; if the artifact does not have any features that differentiate it from others like it, it would not be designated as such. This Buddha statue is not very striking if judged only by its appearance. It is an ordinary run-of-the-mill statue, but it has been

• •

Vairocana Buddha Statue
(National Treasure)

classified as a National Treasure because it was discovered that it is 1300 years old. In addition, its perfectly preserved state provides a great deal of insight into sculptural trends of that period. Artifacts like this one that are old, in perfect condition and have a date of origin that can be proved are eligible to be designated as National Treasures.

If this Buddha statue has a unique feature it is the hands. What is interesting is that one hand is holding the index finger of the other. Many explanations can be used here, but the most widely accepted one is that the world we live in and the world that Buddha lives in are not separate but one and the same. The hand on the bottom probably represents this world while the top hand represents the world inhabited by Buddha. This explanation reflects orthodox Buddhist doctrine. According to Buddhism, it may be easy to think that desire is bad because it is the origin of all pain but it is actually not that different from wisdom. The point here is that the highest form of wisdom does not need to be found elsewhere but can be found within one's own heart. This Buddha statue reminds us of this principle.

Next to the domain of Vairocana Buddha is the domain of Guanyin. This domain is elevated higher than any other domain. This makes the steps leading up to it rather steep. One explanation for the elevated height is that Guanyin lives high up in the mountains. Is it not obvious that a mountain is higher up than other areas? Aside from this, my personal hunch is that Guanyin was placed on such a high pedestal because of her correspondingly high level of popularity. Buddha can be a bit intimidating for a lay Buddhist to approach on any level. He may have too much of a dignified and austere mien for ordinary Buddhists to appeal to and seek at any time. But Guanyin is different. She can be prayed to at any time and asked for any wish at all, all of which she will accept in her boundless compassion. She has a maternal image. Perhaps this is why it is customary to symbolize Guanyin as a woman. The strict and severe Buddha and the compassionate Guanyin-think of these two as the perfect duo of Buddhism.

A legend is passed down in the Buddhism of Silla that illustrates the compassionate nature of Guanyin. There was a monk. One day the county magistrate visited the temple, and the monk became attracted to the magistrate's daughter, who had accompanied her father to the temple. From that day onward, the monk was unable to do anything. At his wit's end, he went before the statue of Guanyin and began to pray. He asked to be able to marry the magistrate's daughter. While he was praying the monk fell asleep. In his dream, the monk married the magistrate's daughter and had a family with her, but the dream did not end well due to various misfortunes like the death of all his children from disease. He then woke up and saw that Guanyin was smiling compassionately down at him. Although it was only a dream, she had granted him his wish. Thereafter, the monk realized that life in this world is in vain and devoted himself to his training. Because this is a famous story, it was even made into a movie in 1990 entitled Dream which was set in Bulguksa.

There is a view from this domain that should not be missed. If you look down from the front of this domain, the scenery that unfolds before your eyes is picture perfect. The sight of the top portion of Dabotap through the roof of the corridor is especially nice. It did not look very large from below, but viewed from here the pagoda seems to soar above its surroundings. It looks like the top rises up from between the roofs. This is as much as there is to be seen in this domain.

What now remains is the domain of Amitabha Buddha or paradise. This domain is the lowest one in Bulguksa. It is said that it was pushed back as a priority because it is where people go after having died. This is not surprising: for the living, isn't this world best? As with the others that we have seen, there is not all that much to see in this domain. The buildings are all recent renovations so they need not be taken too seriously, but the Buddha statue inside *beopdang* is a National Treasure and thus deserves some attention. Made 1300 years ago, it should not be simply bypassed. Nevertheless, we can see that this Buddha statue is not very different from the one that we saw of Vairocana Buddha. The statue's hands are said to be positioned in this way to save various levels of sentient beings but I am not sure of its exact meaning. According to the traditional Buddhist explanation, human beings can overcome fear and achieve what they wish for by looking at Buddha's hands. Of course, there is no way to know for sure whether this is really true or not.

There is only one stone lantern in front of this *beopdang*. The stone lantern is a symbolic object that is supposed to light up the darkness of this world. Thus, there used to also be a stone lantern in front of Main Hall further up. However, there is no pagoda in the Amitabha domain. This is an obvious consequence because

A View Seen of Dabotap from Guanyin Domain

Amitabha Buddha is a being who lives in the imagination; it is thus impossible for there to be physical remains. A being with a physical body like Śākyamuni would, upon being cremated, leave a sari to be placed inside a pagoda, but this does not apply to Amitabha Buddha. The last thing to see here are the steps leading down from the main gate of this domain. As can be seen in the picture, there is a lotus flower carved onto the steps. This is meant to indicate for people to enter by stepping on the flower. It is a representation of a verse from the scriptures stating that one must cross a pond filled with lotus flowers to reach paradise. The soft lines of this flower are made onto hard granite, showing that this sculpture is also that of a highly skilled artisan.

We have now seen everything in Bulkuksa. Let's exit Bulguksa and head to the parking lot. There is a shop outside the Amitabha domain that sells Buddhist souvenir items. Those who wish to purchase souvenirs can do so here — let us now head to our next destination.

5

The name Bulguksa is a transliteration of three Chinese characters: bul, guk and sa. The first two combined denote the actual name of the temple, Bulguk, and the last character means 'temple'. While most books on Korean Buddhist temples that are written in English use the term 'Bulguksa Temple', this book well refer to the temple as Bulguksa as it is done in Korean both for simplicity's sake and to avoid redundancy of the word 'temple'.

6

The original Indian term 'Sākyamuni' was translated into Chinese as 'Seokgamo-ni', the term that is used in Korea today. As is standard in Korean, this book will use the following terms interchangeably: historical Buddha, Sākyamuni, Buddha/Sākyamuni Buddha.

7

Hideyoshi Invasion refers to Japan's invasion of Joseon in 1592. Toyotomi Hideyoshi, in response to the domestic problems within Japan, made the shrewd political decision to counter this and unite public sentiment by invading its neighbor Joseon. The attack was initially successful because of the unprepared and underequipped Joseon army.

A City of the 1000 Years Old Dynasty, Gyeongju

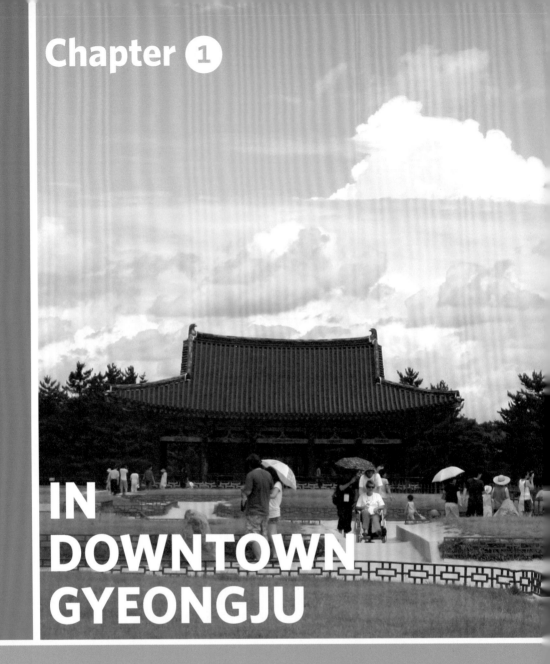

Chapter ❶

IN DOWNTOWN GYEONGJU

Near Wangseong

After having toured Bulguksa and Seokguram Grotto, most people head into the downtown area of Gyeongju. Having once been the site of royal palaces, there is a great deal to see. Also, there are three historic areas registered to UNESCO. Of these three, the one that attracts our attention the most is the royal tombs. Thus, I have said that our tour here will center on the royal tombs, but there is quite a lot to cover before we get to that. There is the Hwangnyongsa site, Bunhwangsa, Wolseong and various other independent artifacts scattered around the vicinity. There is also the Gyeongju National Museum just behind Wolseong, so the city is filled with things to see. I would like to cover them before going to the royal tombs of early Silla, but I do not know how soon this can happen because there is so much to see.

From the ruins of Wangseong   Now we will see (Ban) Wolseong, a royal palace of Silla, but there is not much to explain because only the site that the palace used to be on remains. This city is called either Banweolseong('half-moon fortress') or just Wolseong because it was in the shape of a half moon. If you go see it today, much of the original buildings have collapsed and it simply looks like an ordinary hill because of the large trees now growing on it.

But the discovery of a moat in the northern part of this city in the late twentieth century allowed us to know its boundaries. A moat in this context refers to a small artificial stream that was dug out to block encroachment by enemy armies. The northern moat has since been restored so that it can be opened to public viewing.

Perhaps there should be some clarification about the terms 'palace' and 'city'. The easiest way to understand the layout of Wolseong may be to envision a more famous example of this structure: the Forbidden City in Beijing. It was indeed the home of the emperor - considering only this, it could have been called a palace. But the scale was so large with so many buildings that the name was changed to the word 'city', which suggests the sheer size. Wolseong was organized according to the same system: the unit as a whole is the 'city', while individual buildings inside are known as 'palaces'.

There is not much known historical fact about this city. According to secondary historical sources, all that is known is that it was built in 101 AD as a relatively small palace surrounded by a wall 1.8 kilometers(little over 1 mile) long and that it functioned as the royal palace of Silla until it collapsed in 936. We do not know why Silla built its royal residence here. One point of contention is that it is too small for a royal palace. There were buildings other than this one that were also used as palace buildings, but even adding all of these together does not make it look very large. If you go inside Wolseong today all you will see is a fairly large field with a set of stairs in the middle of it. From a bird's eye view perspective of the city as a whole, the location of this palace is too far south. Building a castle in this type of location is a deviation from the Chinese system, so we can conclude that it was intentionally not built to follow Chinese custom. If the Chinese model had been used in city planning, the city would have been built either in the center of Wanggyeong or at the center of the city's northern boundary. Because this was before Silla began to import Chinese customs, it is estimated that it was built according to native Silla custom. Further inquiry on why the site of the city was established this far south may lead to the explanation that it

● ● Ruined Site of Wolseong

was for better protection of the palace against enemy forces: a look at a map shows that the palace was surrounded by a stream.

While the location may not have followed Chinese custom, the use of mud to build the city wall did follow Chinese style. We may argue that it would have been more appropriate to build with stones because it was the capital city. However, in ancient China mud was preferred over stone when building walls. We may think that a mud wall would not be very strong, but in fact the opposite is true. This is because as long as mud is stacked firmly in layers, no weapon can break through it. For example, a stone wall that is attacked by cannon can collapse in the place that was hit. But mud can resist the attack of any cannonball. But Banwolseong was not built only with mud. Stone was also used; piles of stones can still be seen toward the upper portion of the wall.

When walking along the inside of the wall, you will come across something that looks like a cave. This is a storage room for ice that was used not during Silla but the more recent Joseon dynasty[1392~1910]. The government office that governed the Gyeongju area stored ice here to use for public events or projects. Because there were no refrigerators back then, there was only one way to enjoy ice in the summer. Ice was stored in the winter and eaten in the summer, and a sort of ice refrigerator made of stone was created for this very purpose. The ceiling inside this ice refrigerator is shaped like an arch, which trapped hot air and then released it back outside: this is how the air inside was always kept cool. You can see that there are three ventilators installed at the top. This ice refrigerator is said to have been one of the best in all Joseon, and has since been designated as a Treasure for this reason. It is fascinating that ice that was stored in the winter was able to last until summer. In Joseon, the king only distributed gifts to his high officials on very rare occasions: the day that the king handed out ice was always cause for ecstatic celebration. Ice was that much of a precious gift.

• •
The Ice Refrigerator
Made of Stone
in Wolseong

GYEONGJU, The Heart of Korean Culture

Anapji: The prototype of Korean gardens   Right next to Wolseong, there is a large pond as well as several buildings in the vicinity. Although you of course have to pay an admission fee — there was no admission fee even up to several years ago because it had not been properly renovated back then! — this is Anapji, one of the oldest gardens in Korea. The name 'Anapji' means 'pond of the geese and ducks', but this is not its formal name. The official name of this garden is 'Wolji', or 'Moon Pond'; it is also called 'Imhaejeonji' or 'pond with a building connected to the sea', but I am not sure about the specifics. In the case of Imhaejeonji, the question arises on why the word 'sea' is in the name but the answer to this will be revealed a little later. The stones that are used here were brought over from the seashore as if to create a more ocean-like atmosphere. A fairly large garden, Anapji measures 200 meters^{656ft} east-west and 180 meters^{591ft} north-south, and the stone embankment on which the palace building stands may not seem very long but in fact measures 1 kilometers$^{0.62mile}$ total.

Its function is simple. This building was an auxiliary building of the palace where the crown prince lived and where banquets were held. Historical sources show that it was created in the late seventh century to imitate the natural settings of China. However, this looks very different from Zhuozhengyuan拙政園, a representative Chinese garden located in Suzhou. The inside of Zhuozhengyuan

The Night View of Anapji

is a fascinating spectacle that defies all expression. Every time you turn a corner there is a completely different sight to see. It looks like nature has been uprooted in its entirety and planted in this garden. Compared to this, Anapji has a very simple layout. It is said that Anapji imitates the format of Chinese gardens, but then why does it look so different? This is most likely because in terms of dynasty, Zhuozhengyuan is post Tang while Anapji is Tang; in terms of region, Zhuozhengyuan follows the style of southern gardens while Anapji imitates those of northern China. There are no extant gardens in China that are done in the style of Anapji. But it would probably not be unreasonable to assume that in the Tang dynasty, gardens in the style of Anapji were popular. This was then subsumed by the ornate and highly decorative style of gardens in southern China post Tang as it became increasingly popular.

Then what kind of garden style is Anapji? Generally speaking, it is the harmonious combination of natural beauty and artificial man-made beauty. What does this mean? First of all, as shown in the picture, the part where the palace building is has been marked with a straight line and an embankment has been created with stones. It seems that this part was marked with a straight line because the building had to be there. To indicate the refinement of the royal palace, the embankment was built by stacking neatly cut rectangular stones. Perhaps this is why this reminds us of Gyeonghueru in Gyeongbok

Palace or Buyongji in Changdeok Palace(Refer to my previous book *Soul in Seoul!*). Because these two gardens are royal gardens in which a refined sense of class is crucial, there is a tendency to favor straight lines over curves. This same tendency already shows in the little that we have seen of Anapji. This is why the format of Anapji is called the prototype of Korean gardens.

However, Anapji would not have been worthy of notice if it had only used straight lines. What makes Anapji special is the nature-inspired garden across from the palace. As stated earlier, this garden is an imitation of its Chinese counterpart. To Silla, Chinese culture was not merely a foreign culture but a prototypical universal culture. Thus, imitating it was considered obvious. This 'natural garden' is said to be an imitation of the twelve mountain peaks of Mount Wu, a mountain near the source of the Yangtze River. As I have not yet seen any research that compares Anapji and Mount Wu, I am not sure if this is entirely true. In any case, various mountain tops meet the eye that range between 3 meters$^{9.8ft}$ and 6 meters$^{19.7ft}$ in height. I am not sure as I have not visited Mount Wu, but it is said to be one of the most beautiful scenic spots in all of China.

Along these lines, this pond symbolizes the sea and the part with lots of curving lines is the coast. Why did the people of Silla bring the sea to this garden? This also is a result of Chinese influence, but the ancient Chinese believed that there was an island in

● ● Straight(top) and Curving(bottom) Lines of Anapji

the ocean where immortals lived. Immortals, as the word suggests, are people who never die. The Chinese are one of the few nations in human history who believed that one's physical body could live forever. Not only did they believe that such people really exist but also the fact that they lived on an island that had the elixir of life. Thus, the Chinese made it an ideal to strive for and brought this immortal-inhabited island into the realm of everyday life. In particular, they believed that there were three such islands and then reincorporated this concept into landscaping.

This garden style entered Korea and flourished in Anapji. As a royal garden, Anapji could be designed as large as necessary and this made it possible to include all three islands. Creating an island in the middle of a pond thereafter became standard format for Korean gardens, the prototype of which is found at Anapji. However, Korean gardens of later generations that we find in our midst today are not as large as Anapji and usually only have one island. I have already stated that this garden was designed using the sea as its model. What did Silla landscapers do to make it look like an ocean? Stones from the sea were installed to create a seashore-like atmosphere, but visual effects were also used to physically make this space look like an ocean. Anapji was intentionally designed so that from whichever point it is viewed, the entire pond cannot be seen. Anything that is visible all at once does not look that large. However, by designing

Anapji so that its entirety can never be fully seen, it was made to look much wider than it really is. Instead, only parts of it are visible at a time; the best way to really get a sense of this is to go out on it by boat. In other words, the embankment was built with curving lines to emphasize as natural of an aura as possible and the pond was designed so that a full view of it was only possible by going around it in a boat. The actual boat that was used to travel this pond was discovered at the bottom of the pond(it is perfectly preserved at the Gyeongju National Museum!).

Unfortunately, this beautiful view can only be imagined if you visit Anapji today because this area has not been fully renovated yet. It will probably be difficult if not impossible to fully renovate this because not only did it have all sorts of plants surrounded by a high wall but there were also exotic animals and birds raised on the grounds as well. Of course, there is no way of knowing what kinds of plants or animals were raised here. Also, there is no way of knowing how the wall was built, making a renovation of the original appearance basically impossible at this point. But one thing that is certain is that the original appearance would have been breathtakingly beautiful. With the twelve mountain peaks forming their own ravines and canyons, how extraordinary the entire sight must have been! One factor that allowed this place to look so beautiful was its high wall; with nothing left today except traces of its past, it is not easy to find anything beautiful.

One point to keep in mind here is that the format of this garden became one of the prototypes of Korean gardens of future generations. We have already seen that the stone foundations of the building became a format for the garden culture of the nobility. However, there are far more cases of naturally flowing lines than straight lines in the design of Korean gardens. It can be said that one defining characteristic of Korean gardens is the emphasis placed on natural appearance and the use of artificial human touch as little as possible. In this sense, the natural atmosphere of Anapji can be said to have been the prototype for Korean gardens of future generations. Of course, Anapji is not actually natural but artificially created by human hands from beginning to end. Still, the appearance is very much natural. To sum up, one part of Anapji was created with artificial straight lines while the other was designed with many curving lines that attempt to replicate nature. This is how it attempted to create a harmonious coexistence of humans and nature, and this is also why Anapji is evaluated so highly today.

Regardless of the significance of Anapji within the history of Korean gardens, what is important to us is the location from which the most beautiful view of that garden can be seen. This is because any properly made garden will have a key viewing point that provides the best scenic view of it. In turn, all of the components of the garden are designed for this spot. For example, Buyongji at Changdeok Palace is best seen from a pavilion in the middle of it called Buyongjeong. If we apply the same principle to Anapji, the building from which the most beautiful view can be seen is probably Imhaejeon. This is because many parties were held here. We do not know the exact location of Imhaejeon, but chances are pretty good that it is the large building right in the middle. This may be a purely personal opinion, but I think it has some truth to it because it is the only place from where you can see the incredibly beautiful scenery across the pond all at once. Even inside Imhaejeon, the most important location would be the seat of the guest of honor, but this has yet to be determined.

• •

Buyongji at
Changdeok Palace
in Seoul

In Downtown Gyeongju

Another reason why it is difficult to fully restore Anapji is that it is nearly impossible to revive the sophisticated aesthetic style of the past with the artistic level of modern Koreans. Because they are incapable of restoring the original beauty of Anapji, they try to cover this up by decorating it with outdoor lighting at night. If you visit Anapji at night, all you will see are lights. Gyeongju citizens take great pride in this fact. Not only that, almost all pictures of Anapji online are ones that were taken at night with some of the lotus flowers in the pond. I am not an illumination engineer, but it seems to me that the lighting at Anapji is rather toned-down. I cannot feel the elegance and the high-class atmosphere of the royal court. The lights near the buildings are somewhat acceptable, but those in the western side where the seaside garden is are very strange. I am not saying that having lights at night is wrong in and of itself. I am only trying to say that priorities have not been decided in their proper order. As we have seen earlier, the highlight of Anapji is the garden where there is a harmonious grouping of trees, mountains, stones and animals. This should be properly restored first before adding other decorations like lights; we should not rely entirely on the lighting to salvage the beauty of Anapji.

While doing the research for this book, I found that 26 building complexes have been discovered, meaning that the scale was quite large. As of now, only three complexes have been renovated and the others only have the cornerstones exposed to show that there used to be a building on that spot. The device that pumped water into the pond was also discovered and part of it has survived. There is a lot that can be said about this device, but I will skip the long technical explanation due to lack of page space to conclude that its mechanism is highly scientific. What is truly important about Anapji are the artifacts that were found in the pond. When excavation work began on Anapji in the late 1970s without much expectation of finding anything, they inadvertently hit the jackpot by digging up 30000 artifacts. The artifacts were able to be perfectly preserved without rotting because they were buried inside the soft mud at the bottom of the pond. But what truly makes these artifacts valuable is the fact that they were items actually used in daily life by the people of Silla. Most artifacts that we can see in museums today were excavated from tombs and were thus items meant specifically for display purposes, but the ones found in Anapji were actually used by the royal household. This makes them even more valuable because through them we can get a clear idea of everyday culture in the palace.

Of these artifacts, a selected 700 are currently being displayed in a special annex of the Gyeongju National Museum. It is rare that artifacts from one particular region fill an entire exhibit hall, which further proves the value of these items. We cannot see

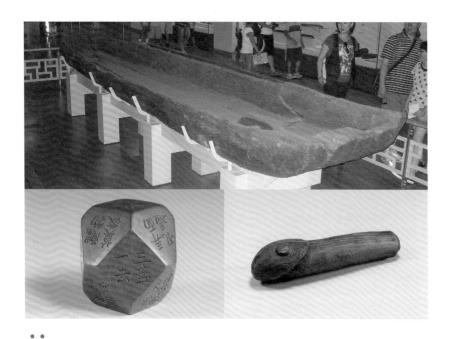

• •

Relics found in Anapji:

Log Boat, Dice and Wooden Phallus ©Gyeongju National Meseum

them all and will have to be satisfied with covering only a few of the more interesting ones. The largest of these artifacts is probably the log boat. Silla royalty would use this boat to travel around the pond and enjoy the beautiful scenery. As you can see in the picture, there is a complicated looking dice. While most die have six sides, this one has eight more to add up to 14. This dice was used when nobles played games. There are characters inscribed on each side, and the game was that you had to roll the dice and then do whatever was

GYEONGJU, The Heart of Korean Culture

inscribed on the upturned side. For example, if a side comes up that says 'Drink three shots(all at once)', the person would have to drink three shots of alcohol on the spot. There are various other amusing punishments, including 'get your nose hit by everyone else', 'do not move even if your face feels ticklish', 'dance without music', etc.

Even more interesting than this dice are the wooden phalluses as can be seen in the photograph. One noteworthy feature is the fact that they look disturbingly realistic. Whenever these types of artifacts are found, there is always a debate as to whether women actually used them or not. Those who say that they were not actually used argue that the wood material would have been too hard and thus unsuitable for use. Instead, they suggest that the phalluses were only kept as fertility symbols. On the other hand, those who say that these were actually used use the reason that they are extremely life-like representations of the male sex organ. Although no agreement has been reached, the latter seems more probable when considering that these phalluses were owned by court ladies who lived in the palace. This is because a court lady was forbidden from having sexual relations with a man for her entire life.

Fallen remains of royal temples:
Looking around the site of
Hwangnyongsa and Bunhwangsa

If you go a little farther up from Anapji you will see a wide lot and a small temple. This is one of the Gyeongju Historic Areas registered by UNESCO: the Hwangnyongsa · Bunhwangsa District. There is not a great deal to say about this area because not much from its past has survived. But these two temples have nevertheless been registered as world heritage items despite the fact that only the site remains because they were very important temples in the past, Hwangnyongsa in particular. Perhaps this is why there is a miniature version of Hwangnyongsa on display at Gyeongju National Museum as shown in the picture. The main attraction of this temple is of course the nine-story wooden pagoda. A wooden pagoda is not a very big deal; it has the exact same structure as a Chinese-style house. The only difference is that it is built slightly taller. Because this pagoda is the most famous feature of this temple, a brief explanation of the pagoda will suffice for our purposes.

The temple itself was built in the mid-sixth century and was a royal temple. Because it was in charge of all religious ceremonies of the royal court, it was extremely large in scale. It is said that the temple measured 288 meters[approx. 945ft] east-west and 281 meters[approx.

[922ft] north-south: you can imagine just how big it was. There are stories that it was the largest temple in the East, but this probably is not true. The pagoda was built a full century after the temple in the mid-seventh century during the reign of Queen Seondeok, the first female king of Silla.[8] This pagoda well exceeds other pagodas beginning with its size. With a height of 80 meters [262.5ft] and composed of nine stories, it was an extremely tall pagoda. Thus, it is said that there was no place in downtown Gyeongju from where this pagoda was not visible. It never ceases to amaze me that such a tall structure was built entirely out of wood with no concrete, but there was no technician in Silla at that time who could accomplish this feat. Instead, an architect had to be brought in from neighboring Baekje, which shows how advanced the technology was in the latter. Baekje at the time had absorbed cutting-edge technology from southern China, but Silla had no such advantages as a kingdom in the far corner of the peninsula. As can be seen in the photograph, if you visit here today there is nothing that remains except for the cornerstones on which the pillars stood. Seeing how densely set these cornerstones are, we can infer that many pillars were needed to support the extra weight of this tall building.

Why did Queen Seondeok build such a tall pagoda? Interestingly there were three female kings in the thousand year history of Silla. Among all the dynasties in Korean history, Silla is the only one

The Miniature Model of Hwangnyongsa(top)
The Site of Hwangnyongsa(bottom)

in which a woman was able to become king, and Queen Seondeok was the first of these. As the first female king, Queen Seondeok not only received constant ridicule from neighboring countries but Silla also suffered frequent foreign attacks as well. Once when a Silla emissary paid a visit to the Tang court, the Tang emperor criticized the fact that Seondeok was a woman and derisively asked whether he should send a Chinese man to act as a proper king. There was another case in which a sitting prime minister raised a coup that she was barely able to stamp out. Under these circumstances, Queen Seondeok would have felt a dire need to strengthen her authority, and one result of this was this pagoda. When considering this in proportion to the other buildings in the temple or the area of the temple as a whole, the pagoda is far too big. For a pagoda of this stature, the courtyard should have been much wider. From within the temple, it would probably have been impossible to see its top even by bending your head all the way back. This is the extent to which Queen Seondeok tried to build the pagoda as tall as humanly possible so that she could strengthen the basis of her authority. Whatever the exact situation was, it is unfortunate that we do not know the original layout of this pagoda. Because it was so tall it was often hit by lightning. The damages of this were only partial and thus quickly renovated, but this pagoda finally disappeared from history when it was burned to the ground in the Mongol invasion during the Goryeo dynasty in 1238.

While the pagoda is the most important feature of this temple, the *beopdang* of this temple required a few words of qualification as well. This is because the only piece of this building that remains is one roof tile. As shown in the photograph, this was not a typical roof tile; it was placed at either edge of the roof and designed so that it could make the building look more dignified and high-class rather than having any practical function. But the problem is the size of this roof tile. Currently on display at the Gyeongju National Museum, it is a shocking 182 centimeters^{approx. 6ft} high. We can estimate how large this *beopdang* would have been judging from the size of this roof tile: slightly over 1000 people would have been able to fit inside. It was a truly formidable size befitting of a royal temple. There are no *beopdang* in Korea today that are anywhere near this large. Because Buddhism was persecuted all throughout the Joseon dynasty, there would have been no resources available to build a *beopdang* of this size.

This roof tile has one interesting feature. If you look closely at the middle part of the tile, you can see that a human face has been drawn in a very comical manner. Only a few simple lines were used to draw a laughing expression on the face. One thing we must keep in mind here is that as a stern and solemn royal temple, little 'jokes' like this would have been prohibited. This picture was prob-

A Roof Tile of Hwangnyongsa

ably carved in by the artisan who created this temple and this type of humor is found in Silla clay figurines as well. It is nearly impossible to find examples of these types of pranks in places as important as the royal temple in neighboring China or Japan, but Koreans enjoy it in a variety of settings. The tiger painting that you see here is a representative example. There are probably not many nations in the world that would depict a tiger in such a comic manner; this example shows that Koreans have a deep affinity with comedy. This mentality has been passed down intact to the present day, in which the three major Korean television networks compete fiercely over weekend evening comedy program timeslots. I do not think that there

Comical Human Face
in the middle of the
Hwangnyongsa Roof Tile(top)

Comical Tiger on a
Porcelain of the Joseon
period (bottom)

are many countries in the world where comedy programs are this popular.

Lastly, you will see three rather large stones in the place that the Buddha statue was located within this *beopdang*. It was reputed to be over 5 meters^{approx. 16.4ft} tall, meaning that it was an exceedingly tall statue. Now we have basically seen all that there is to see of this temple. Even if you wish to see more, it is impossible to do so because only the site of the building remains. We will now move over to Bunhwangsa, which can be done by walking because it is right across the street.

This temple also does not have a great deal to see because all that remains today is a pagoda and two or three buildings. But it was not always like this. Along with Hwangnyongsa, this temple was also a very important temple in Silla. Records stating that the Buddha statue here was approximately eight times larger than the one at Hwangnyongsa attest to the importance of Bunhwangsa. Also, many famous monks spent time here at one point or another. The one among these that deserves our attention is Wonhyo. Wonhyo is recognized as the greatest person ever in the entire history of Korean religion. There are countless anecdotes that praise his greatness, but his most important accomplishment is that he was not only one of the greatest Buddhist thinkers in East Asia of his day but was also the most prominent activist of popular religion. His life story itself illustrates the kind of person that a great religious thinker should be. On his way to study abroad in China, the center of Buddhist doctrine, he was profoundly enlightened and returned to Silla. There are countless books in his name, the scholarship of which exceeds China. To give a small example of this, the most eminent monk of the Huayan School in China would write to Wonyo whenever he became stuck while annotating the *Avatamska Sutra*. Even aside from this, it is said that Chinese monks referred to many other of Wonhyo's works, which proves the depth of his scholarship.

But Wonhyo, as befitting a religious thinker, did not only spend his time researching religious scriptures. Believing that he needed to save the souls of Silla citizens by proselytizing Buddhism to them, he defrocked himself and went out into lay society. He wore clothes like everyone else, grew out his hair and sang and danced to songs about the profound truth of Buddhism. He invited people who were completely ignorant to Buddhism by teaching them to say 'I sincerely believe in Amitabha^{Namu Amitabhabul}'. As is well-known, the Pure Land School^{Kor. Jeongtojong, Sansk. Sukkāvatī} believes that you will be reborn in paradise after death if you recite the phrase 'Namu Amitabhabul' ten times. This type of simple teaching was essential to ordinary people for whom Buddhist doctrine was too difficult to understand. Wonhyo actually put this into action. Thanks to his efforts at proselytizing, Buddhism spread throughout all of Silla.

As we have seen so far, the greatness of Wonhyo lies in the fact that he combined theory and practice better than any thinker had done so before him. Most religious thinkers only focus on only one aspect, but Wonhyo transcended this limitation. There is another interesting quality about Wonhyo. After he left the temple to enter the world of the common people, Wonhyo spent a few nights with a noblewoman of high social class. He declared that this was his breaking of his vows and thereafter entered secular society. The great individual who resulted from this union is Seolchong, the luminary of Korean Confucianism. In other words, Seolchong is considered the starting point of Confucianism in Korea. Can you now see how important this father, the most important Buddhist monk, and son, the origin of Korean Confucianism, are within the flow of Korean philosophy? Many stories are thus told about Wonhyo, and the place where he spent his later years and eventually died is Bunhwangsa. For this, a portrait of Wonhyo is still on display here. This portrait was of course created recently based purely on imagination. How could we know what someone who lived in Silla looked like?

Apart from these stories, another feature of this temple that we should focus on is the pagoda of which only three floors remain. It looks rather different from Seokgatap which we saw earlier because it is not made of stone but brick. But if you look closely, you can see that it is not really brick. The material is not actually brick but stone that was cut to look like brick. Why was this done? The brick pagoda is a style that was actually highly popular in China. Having imported Buddhist culture from China, Silla of course imported the brick pagoda style and created several brick pagodas themselves. This pagoda is one result of this; interestingly, it has been created from stones cut in the shape of bricks rather than actual bricks. This makes this pagoda a rarity for which it has been designated as a National Treasure. However, we do not know for sure how many floors there originally used to be because of several improperly done renovations. The estimate is seven or possibly nine stories.

The real fun of looking at this pagoda lies not in the stolid construction of the pagoda itself but the statues of people carved into the door or the foundation platform. As you can see in the picture, the natural uncut appearance of the stones that have been fitted together in their original shape adds a nice touch. Judging also from the stone steps at Bulguksa that we saw earlier, this style must have

The Three-Story Pagoda in Bunhwangsa

been frequently used in Silla at that time. Most tourists are not very interested in the foundation, but I personally think that there is more that greets the eye here than the heavy and stocky-looking pagoda.

This concludes our tour of Bunhwangsa. There are other various miscellaneous details but these can be seen on the signboards at the temple. There is one more interesting episode that I would like to share about Bunhwangsa that has to do with the pond in the back of the temple. If you go to Gyeongju National Museum today you can see in the backyard many Buddha statues with their heads cut off; these were originally found in this pond. We do not know for sure why these decapitated Buddha statues were found inside this particular pond. The hypothesis is that during the Joseon dynasty when persecution of Buddhism was at its zenith, students at the local Confucian academy gathered all the Buddha statues they could find, cut the heads off and dumped them into this pond. Even after being heavily persecuted by Confucianism, Buddhism did not disappear from history and a complete reversal has taken place today in that Buddhism is now much more popular. The influence of Buddhism continues to grow, but that of Confucianism is gradually losing its foothold within Korean society. The discussion on the future of Korean Confucianism is no doubt a very important one, but let's leave it for later and now head to Daeneungwon.

The Road to Daeneungwon:
Cheomseongdae and Gyerim

While walking toward Daeneungwon on the road that goes back to Anapji, you will encounter a strange-looking stone structure. This is Cheomseongdae, what Koreans proudly believe to be the oldest astronomical observatory in the East. However, this is a slightly problematic claim in that to this day, not even the exact function of this building has been agreed upon. The crux of the debate over Cheomseongdae is the argument over whether it really was an observatory or whether it was merely a symbolic structure that was built near a larger observatory facility. Most experts agree that it was not symbolic but actually had a role in observing the sky.

There did not even used to be an admission fee for Cheomseongdae because it was simply out by itself in the middle of an empty field. I remember when I first visited Gyeongju in 1964 that there were small thatched-roof houses all around it and the entire scene was like any typical farming village. It is said that there used to be a wall around Cheomseongdae, which is not surprising at all when considering how important this building is. But even if we accept the fact that this was really used as an observatory, the problem is that neither the appearance of the building nor any of its other features(height, etc.) look like they have anything to do with observing the sky. If it was a really observatory, it should be located high up in the mountains or at least be very tall; Cheomseongdae does not have any of these characteristics. Also, the top of the structure looks too narrow for a person to have been able to do anything from it. Because of this, there have always been numerous theories: the building was a sort of sundial, it was merely a mathematical symbol, it symbolized Mount Sumi, the mountain at the center of the world in Buddhism, etc. As seen in these varied hypotheses, it is difficult to establish the function of this building. But one thing clear is that in one way or another, this place was used as an observatory.

• • Cheomseongdae in 1964

••
The Middle part of
Cheomseongdae

This conclusion can be derived from the following. As can be seen in the picture, the middle portion of Cheomseongdae has a hole in it; this is to hang a ladder on either side so that people can go in and out. After coming inside the building after having reached this point via ladder, the person could then climb to the top and observe the sky from there. Thus, it is true that observation could actually be done.

But why did the people of Silla observe the sky? The answer to this question has to do with the philosophy of ancient people on nature. According to the ancient worldview, nature was not separate but a single entity with human beings and thus it interfered in the lives of the latter. In order to know the intentions of nature, they believed that it had to always be observed. For example, natural disasters like flood or famine were interpreted as punishment for improper governance by the king. Being careful about one's actions and words during a solar or lunar eclipse also falls into this logic. Aside from this type of superstitious interpretation, being able to predict the weather was essential to an agrarian society. Ancient people had two purposes for observing the stars: 1) to predict the future of the country and 2) to create calendars. Thus, to them observing the sky was a big priority.

Those who argue that Cheomseongdae was an astronomical observatory point to various convincing pieces of evidence to back up their claims. One of them is rather symbolic in nature in that 361.5 stones were used for this building or that there are 27 or 28 layers of stones in total. Here the 361.5 stones symbolize the number of days in a year; the number of layers is more symbolic. First of all, 27 layers indicate the number of units that make up the body and is also related to the fact that Queen Seondeok is the 27th king of Silla. If we add the square-shaped structure at the top, it adds up to 28 layers total; 28 is the number of divisions of Chinese constellations. The ancient Chinese divided up the sky into 28 sections to classify the constellations.

There are other symbolic explanations aside from these related to aspects of the weather, but I will exclude these because I feel that they are specious explanations that can be altered at will to fit the situation. But the conclusion remains that this place was used for observation purposes, as does the question of why it had to be this particular location. The answer can probably be found if people actually try observing the stars here for about a year. We are now going to leave Cheomseongdae, but before we do so I will introduce a source for those readers who want to know more about what we have just discussed. The Silla Arts and Science Museum has a miniature mock-up of what it would have looked like to observe the stars from Cheomseongdae which helps understand the process a lot better.

Before going to Daeneungwon, there is an artifact just in front of Wolseong called Gyerim. The direct translation of this word would be 'forest of chicken'. It is the site of a legend that is related to the Silla king. There was a total of approximately 50 kings in Silla, and while most of them had the last name Kim there were several in early Silla who had other last names(The person who established Silla was not a Kim but a Park!). The Kim clan began to exercise a monopoly over the throne from the mid-fourth century. From then until the tenth century, almost all kings were Kims. Gyerim is the place according to legend where the patriarch of the Kim clan came down from the sky. The legend goes something like this: one morning long ago, the sound of a chicken crowing was heard. Upon following the sound, people found a golden chest caught in the branches of a tree. Interestingly, a white chicken was crowing under the tree. When the golden chest was opened, a boy walked out; this child is Kim Alji, the Kim clan patriarch. As this occurred in the mid-first century, we can see that it took 300 years for the Kim clan to completely dominate the Silla throne.

While there are many hypotheses about exactly who these Kims were, most agree that they migrated to the peninsula from abroad. It is also estimated that they were a highly advanced people who were much better at horseriding and had more developed smelting technology than indigenous people in the Silla region. It is also possible to extrapolate that given that the Chinese character for the name 'Kim' means 'gold' in Chinese, they were also skilled at gold metalwork; the fact that the child emerged from a crate made of gold is in the same context. Also, we will observe this more carefully later on but the gold crowns that were the pride of Silla were all worn by kings of the Kim clan. Obviously there is a special connection between members of the Kim lineage and gold. This gold crown was discovered in a large royal tomb at our next destination, Daeneungwon. This is where the Kims, the kings of early Silla, are buried. These large mounded tombs began to be used in the fourth century as members of the Kim clan ascended the throne.

However, while the connection between this legend and early Silla history seems to be legitimate, there is not much to see here today apart from a few trees and a small house. As the place where the patriarch of the Silla kings came into being, I think that the area should somehow be decorated to deliver the story that makes it so significant. It is not right for visitors to be left to their own devices as they are now. I wonder what the Gyeongju Kims think about leaving abandoned the birthplace of their most important ancestor.

Five minutes is plenty of time to walk from here to Daeneungwon. It is a pleasant walk because of the large tombs along the way and the well-trimmed grass. The large tombs definitely house people who had very high social status, but we do not know who they are. Once you pass this path and cross the road you will see the Daeneungwon parking lot, which is hectic because there are always so many cars. Supposedly it cannot be helped because of the many visitors that come to see a world heritage item, but I still cannot help feeling that this whole area should be better organized somehow. But once you enter Daeneungwon it is much nicer and quieter because it has been decorated like a park. Let's continue on toward Daeneungwon.

The term 'Queen Seondeok' is actually misleading because 'queen' is technically the title given to the wife of a king. However, Queen Seondeok was not anyone's wife but was herself a king - thus, a female king. Because while a term for 'female king(*yeowang*)' exists in Korean, there is no English equivalent, most books including this one refer to Seondeok as 'Queen' Seondeok for lack of a better translation.

INSIDE THE ROYAL TOMBS OF SILLA: The treasure chest of Silla culture

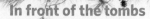

In front of the tombs

Looking at artifacts from the tombs

The expression 'city of gold' is often used when describing Silla, and this is because there is an extremely beautiful gold crown that was found here. Then where did the crown come from? The obvious answer is that it came from a grave. These glittering ornate crowns were discovered in the tombs of Silla kings that are all over downtown Gyeongju. In these tombs are not only gold crowns but an immense quantity of very unique artifacts. It is also where exotic artifacts that entered via the Silk Road from Central Asia were discovered. This is why these royal tombs are called the treasure chest of Silla culture. It is also rare that there are so many tombs in the downtown area of a city. Because they are the first thing that first-time visitors to Gyeongju notice and also what they end up seeing the most often, tombs are like the landmark of Gyeongju. Because of this and various other reasons, Daeneungwon and the tombs around it have been registered as UNESCO world heritage items. Items that are currently registered as World Heritages include a number of royal tombs from the Joseon dynasty as well; this shows that Korea as a nation is very interested in tombs generally. In this chapter we will observe not only the tombs themselves but also spend a great deal of time looking at the artifacts excavated from these tombs. This is because the secret of Silla culture can oftentimes be found from these artifacts. Let's first look at the tombs.

In front of the tombs

We are now at the entrance to Daeneungwon. Because the immediate area is too full of stores and cars moving around, let's head inside the park. This actually was not the type of park that is gated and has an admission fee. As with everything else in Gyeongju, they were simply tombs that happened to be in the middle of the downtown area. This was changed into the park that it is today in 1973. It was probably due to the flood of tourists, but I sometimes wonder what it looked like before. This is purely a guess on my part, but would it not have looked so much more beautiful than it does today? But because I do not remember a great deal of my childhood visit to Gyeongju, I only have the faintest of recollections about what the former appearance looked like.

I am able to have such thoughts about its former beauty because of the stories I heard from elderly adults. This is already a very old story, but one gentleman told me that he once brought a German guest to Gyeongju. This German then looked only at the tombs for one or two hours before asking to return to Seoul. When he asked his guest why he wanted to go back without having seen anything else in Gyeongju, the German replied that 'Just having seen this is enough. The harmony of the mountains and the tombs is the epitome of beauty; it is not good to see something good too much'. As the

• • Tombs seen around Gyeongju

German pointed out, this probably looked much more beautiful a long time ago but this is no longer true today. This is because it has been damaged in various ways due to having become a playground for children, etc. While I can understand the desire of the Gyeongju city government to prevent further damage to these tombs by making the area a park, it is still a huge pity that it has lost its original appearance.

There are two main categories of tombs in Gyeongju: those that are on flat land and those on hills. The tombs registered with UNESCO are those on flat land, which are the tombs that are within a 1km east-west radius and 1.5 kilometers north-south radius with Daeneungwon at the center. There are also tombs on hills out the outskirts of Gyeongju, but we will not cover them here. An entire book would be insufficient when covering each of these one by one, so we will only cover the ones that are registered with UNESCO. This is how plentiful tombs are in Gyeongju. In fact, there is no way of knowing exactly how many old tombs are in Gyeongju because oftentimes the dirt collapses downward and thus loses the appearance of a tomb or they are located underground so that there is no way of seeing it. For example, while fixing the upkeep of the large tombs here in Daeneungwon, countless smaller tombs were found underground. There is no way of knowing the exact statistic because there are so many cases like this.

The literal translation of the word 'Daeneungwon' is 'park with large tomb'. But because there is not only one tomb but countless scores of them, only a tiny minority knows which tomb belongs to who. All we know now is that these tombs are from before the fifth century during the era that the Kim clan dominated the throne. The newly coronated Kims built large tombs like this in order to show off their power.

Tombs that cannot be robbed: The secret of Silla royal tombs

As I stated earlier, countless artifacts have emerged from Silla tombs. This was possible due to their unique structure and layout. Let's find out by looking at this diagram. To see what it actually looks like, you can visit Cheonmachong, the only tomb in this park that has been opened to reveal the inside. First of all, after the body is placed inside the coffin, the coffin is then placed inside a huge wooden crate. Many artifacts are placed next to the coffin. The lid of the crate is then closed and a stone the size of a human head is placed on top of it. Above this stone, clay is tightly packed in order to prevent rainwater from seeping in. Next, this is covered with a layer of dirt to

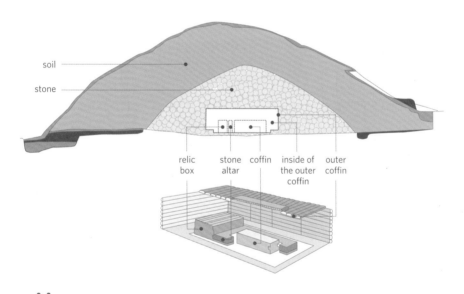

soil
stone

relic box | stone altar | coffin | inside of the outer coffin | outer coffin

Structure of the tomb of Silla kings
©Myunghun Lee

form the shape of a tomb. Silla tombs are so large because they have undergone many steps like these.

However, this format did not last for very long because the wooden crate would rot and collapse. This then causes stones and dirt to enter and fill in the inside of the crate. This makes it very difficult for graverobbers, who would have to dig out all the accumulated stones and dirt. Graverobbers by necessity have to work at night, but it is nearly impossible to finish digging out all the dirt and stones in one night without making a sound. It is a process that takes weeks even for an official excavation with all of the proper machinery; thus, it is unthinkable task for gravediggers. By being able to be preserved in this way, Silla tombs survived into the present day and were registered as world heritage items.

There is one problem that constantly surfaces when dealing with Silla tombs, and that is the question of where this tomb style originated from. This tomb format is not found in other parts of the peninsula and only in downtown Gyeongju. This is what causes questions about its origins to arise. But there was an incident that received the undivided attention of academics: a similar tomb format was discovered far from the Korean peninsula in northern Siberia and its surrounding regions. The problem is that this format is only found in Gyeongju and Siberia and no other regions in between these two. We do not know what kind of exchange there had been between these two regions or by what path this tomb format was sent along. Had this format been passed along via land, there should be examples of it all along the path that was taken but none have been discovered. Regardless, this mystery has recently begun to show signs of clearing up. A new hypothesis argues that the ancestors of the royal Silla Kim clan were the Huns. If this is true, it could be probable that the Huns brought this tomb style with them when they entered the peninsula. Because the descendents of the Huns entered the peninsula not via land but via a sea route from Northeast China, it may be reasonable that the grave memorial service is not found in other regions of Korea.

There is other evidence that also supports the hypothesis that it was the nomadic Huns who entered the Korean peninsula. As you can see in this picture, a clay plate was found in one of the tombs near Daeneungwon. Because it is in the shape of a man riding a horse it may not seem like one, but the structure is definitely that of a bowl. The bowl that is behind the sitting man is where water goes in and the spout beneath the horses's head is where water flows out. What interests us is this object as a whole. This is a bronze pot that was a favorite item of nomadic tribes. These people were always on the move, and so they carried the pot around with them. If they stop somewhere, this pot would be hung onto something before being used to cook. This is why it is immediately obvious that whenever

194

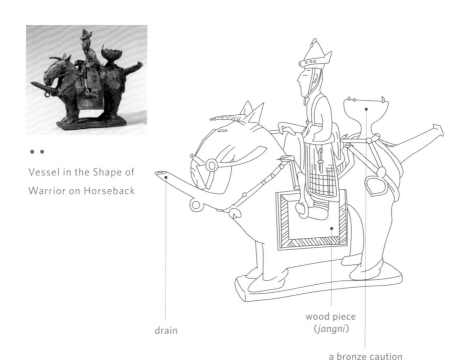

Vessel in the Shape of
Warrior on Horseback

drain

wood piece
(*jangni*)

a bronze caution

this pot comes out, it is somehow related to nomadic people and that the royal families of early Silla were descended from nomadic culture. The early royal families most likely believed that they were descendents of the Huns.

Into the tombs   The only tomb in this park that is open for public viewing is Cheonmachong. It is the only tomb in Gyeongju into which you can actually go inside, and the name means 'tomb(with drawings) of the flying horse'. The name is derived from a wood piece found inside the tomb that had a drawing of a flying horse on it. It is believed to be the tomb of a king but because we do not know which king it was, the name of the tomb reflects not the king's name but the name of a specific artifact. The wood piece was placed underneath the saddle so that mud would not splash onto the rider's clothing when riding a horse. This artifact shows that the people of Silla were closely related to the nomadic tribes who were expert horseriders. One interesting fact about this drawing is that it is one of the only ones from Silla that remain. Because it has been 1000 years since the collapse of Silla, there are no paintings or drawings that have survived to the present day. This drawing is particularly valuable because only those that were placed in tombs like this one were able to survive.

• •
Inside of Cheonmachong

GYEONGJU, The Heart of Korean Culture

The Drawing of a Flying Horse found in Cheonmachong
©National Meseum of Korea

One good thing about this tomb is that the inside of it has been replicated. A cross-section is displayed so that you can see exactly how the tomb was constructed. We have already discussed the format of this tomb in an earlier section, but it is made even more realistic here because the appearance of the inside at the time of its excavation has been perfectly recreated. Of course the corpse is no longer here but other artifacts like the gold crown and gold belt are all on display. Artifacts that are found in tombs like this one are worth seeing because they tend to have many unique features; this is especially true of the countless gold items that are found including the gold crown, the most representative artifact of Silla culture. We will take a closer look at this crown later on because it is so important. There are then artifacts from Central Asia that also deserve our attention. Strangely enough, of the three kingdoms on the peninsula at that time, it is only in Silla that Central Asian artifacts that came over on the Silk Road are found. Of these, there are not a few that are from Rome. We discussed this briefly in the introduction and will discuss it again in further detail later. Of the many interesting artifacts here, let's first look at the most representative piece: the gold crown.

Looking at artifacts from the tombs

Silla, the kingdom of gold: The gold crown   As you can tell from the fact that many kings had a last name which means 'gold', Silla was a nation that was closely related to gold. As I briefly mentioned at the beginning, the words of the eminent ninth century Persian geographer Ibn Khurdadhibah[820~912] that 'a country at the end of China has a great deal of gold, and Muslims do not come back after they have gone there because they enjoy it so much' are telling. Another interesting fact is that there is a Chinese dynasty whose name means 'gold', the Jin dynasty[1115~1234]. The Chinese character that is used here, '*geum*', is the same as the one used in Korea to spell 'Kim'. The fact that this dynasty was named after gold is closely related to Silla because it was established by descendants of the Silla royal family who moved to Manchuria after Silla collapsed. Thus, they simply used their own name to name the dynasty(The last dynasty of China, Qing, was established by a descendant of Jin, which further suggests the close relationship between China and Korea).

If you observe the various gold artifacts you will see that Silla was much more skilled than its neighbors in terms of gold metalwork: how was this possible? This is most likely because the people who migrated to Silla were skilled at gold metalworking. If you go to the Gyeongju National Museum, you can still see gold

The Golden Crown found in 'Royal Tomb of Golden Crown'
©Gyeongju National Meseum

earrings, necklaces, bracelets as well as countless other decorative items. But while gold decorations are found in other countries as well, the gold crown is different because it is only found in Silla.

The Silla gold crown is unique even among the various gold crowns of ancient civilizations. Not only are the aesthetic beauty and metalwork technology highly developed but a relatively large number of them are extant today. It is said that of the gold crowns preserved by antiquity, the ones from Silla comprise over half of them: this in and of itself is an unparalleled feat. Out of approximately twelve ancient gold crowns, six or seven are from Silla, making it over half. In addition, the gold metalwork technology of Silla surpassed that of any other people. However, these beautiful gold crowns were uncovered and revealed for the first time as late as 1921. Because of a long-held belief among Koreans that digging up someone else's grave would bring huge misfortune, no one had thought to dig up these graves. If this was true of ordinary graves, royal graves were even further avoided.

On top of this, this first gold crown was excavated from a tomb that people had not even known was a tomb because the dirt covering it had all completely collapsed. Thus people did not realize until the twentieth century that Silla had created such magnificent crowns. It all began in 1921 when a Gyeongju resident stumbled upon the grave while digging the site of his home. This tomb was discovered not in Daeneungwon but in the grave district right next to it^{Nodongdong-Noseodong}. Because it is next to Daeneungwon, it is estimated that this was also the burial site of early Silla kings or their close relatives. News soon reached the Japanese colonial government who was charge at that time, and excavation work was immediately begun. Whether it was because they did not care much about artifacts found in a mere colony or they simply started right in without any plans, excavation was completed within just four days. When I reflect on it now, I realize that these tombs should not have been excavated in this way. Without a great deal of planning and attention to detail in the excavation process, there is a high chance that the artifacts will be damaged. This shows to some extent how problematic the cultural policy of the Japanese government was at the time. In any case, the first gold crown is excavated from this tomb. We can infer that this was a king's tomb because of the crown, we do not know this king's name because there are no records that remain about tombs. Thus, all tombs that were excavated thereafter were named according to a unique feature or episode of that tomb. Because this is where the first gold crown was discovered it was named Royal Tomb of Golden Crown.

It is said that there were a lot of foreign substances on the surface of the crown when it was first excavated. However, after cleaning it, the original appearance of 1500 years ago came through perfectly. Even after so many centuries had passed it was soon able to recover its original splendor. The gold crown that we can see at the museum looks exactly the way it originally did, which is what makes it such a precious entity. This is why people all throughout history have always been captivated by gold. The constant and unchanging nature of the substance appealed to people. But the gold crown really receives the spotlight for its overall fancy appearance and the high degree of metalwork. The latter is probably what made the fancy and ornate appearance possible. As you can see in the picture, the gold crown looks from the front like tree branches and deer antlers from the side. Onto these were attached comma-shaped jade pieces and round pieces of gold, composing the basic format of the gold crown. While all gold crowns follow the same basic structure, they look slightly different depending on whether they are highly decorated or not.

But the problem here is the style of these crowns. There is still plenty of debate among scholars about the origin of this style because it has not yet been found in any other country. Let's briefly look into this debate to gain a better understanding of the gold crown and the people of Silla. The hypothesis that has the most supporters states that the gold crown was adapted from the crown worn by Siberian shamans. This is understandable if we assume, as stated earlier, that the kings of Silla are descendants of the northern Huns. The shaman's crown is identical to that of the tribe chief because in ancient Hun society, the shaman and chief was believed to be the same person. From this perspective, the various decorations on the crown make sense as well. First of all, the tree branch design mentioned earlier is the divine tree that connected this world to the heavens. There are seven branches because shamans at that time believed that the sky was composed of seven floors and the branches are a representation of this idea. The deer antlers on the sides represent the animal that the shaman rides to go to heaven. The deer was believed to have superpowers and have a special messenger role in going back and forth between this world and heaven. Remnants of this belief about deer are found today: the reindeer that lead Santa's sleigh all over the world in a single night are believed to be supernatural.

Other decorations are added to the crown as well; the most common of these are the bird wings. If these wings are fastened in the front of the crown, it looks much more dignified and regal. But why bird wings? Ancient societies at that time used the feather of a large bird in funeral ceremonies because it was believed that this feather would send the soul up to heaven. It was probably the shaman who sent the soul to heaven on the feather. Scholars argue that because the feather is connected to the shaman, the entire crown should be connected to the shaman's identity as well.

Another hypothesis suggests that the connection between

204

GYEONGJU, The Heart of Korean Culture

the kings of early Silla and the shaman can be seen from the golden belt. As you can see in the picture, there are about 20 decorations hung on this belt like charms on a charm bracelet. They include a variety of shapes like a fish, knife, glass bottle, whetstone and curved jade; some say that these were tools used by a shaman to cure illnesses while others say that they were tools carried around by nomadic people. If it is difficult to imagine all of these actually hanging from a belt, think of the tool belt worn by mechanics today. Whatever the truth is, scholars argue that these artifacts signify a connection to nomadic people in some way. Thought about in this way, it seem quite reasonable that Silla kings were related to northern nomadic tribes or shamans.

Plenty more stories can be told about the gold crown, but let me share one final story before I finish. There is some debate about whether the Silla king actually wore this gold crown. There are two main arguments here, but let's first consider the one that this crown was not actually used but only applied as an accessory after the king had died. According to supporters of this argument, the crown would not be able to hold up its own weight if it were actually worn because of the weight of the jade and gold pieces. This seems reasonable because gold is such a pliable metal that when spread out very thinly it has a hard time standing by itself. But the Silla gold crown has added jade and gold pieces to this thin gold, so

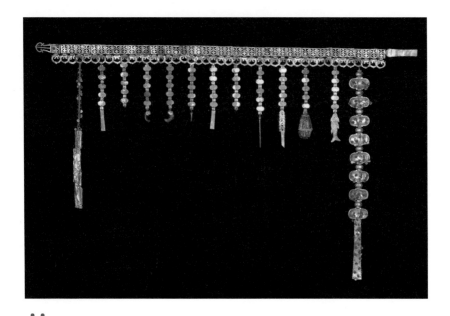

The Golden belt found in Cheonmachong ©Gyeongju National Meseum

the question remains as to how this was possible. Also, if the crown was actually worn, there should be traces of silk or leather lining the inside rim of the crown but there are none. This proves the argument that the crown was not actually worn by the king. Lastly, it is said that the appearance of the crown upon excavation itself shows that it was not worn. When the tomb was first opened up, the crown was found not on the body's head but placed on the lips. This shows that the crown was indeed an accessory and not actually worn.

Those who refute this hypothesis argue that while the crown may not have been worn by the king on a daily basis, it would have been worn for special occasions. In response to the argument that the gold could not withstand the weight of the ornaments they state that special techniques would have been used to prevent the gold from collapsing. To get an idea of this, let's look at the edges of a crown that is standing by itself. There are many holes drilled along the edges; they say that the gold is then strengthened by these holes and is able to withstand more weight. Although it looks quite simple it is said to be a highly refined technology which allows the crown to stand by itself. Also, the gold pieces moved together with the crown when it was actually worn and so they say that it was worn just to see this spectacle. I personally would like to follow this hypothesis because wearing the crown would have showed off the king's authority. The sight of the king wearing the gold crown and belt would have been awe-inspiring. It is difficult to believe that such a fine and ornate crown and belt would be created only to take it to the grave without having ever worn it.

This finishes our review of the gold crown, but one point I would like to reiterate is that not all Silla kings wore the gold crown. After adopting Chinese court dress in the seventh century, much of the indigenous Silla attire stops being worn thereafter. Thus, the gold crown also stops being created and is not found in tombs that are created after the seventh century.

As I stated at the beginning of this book, Silla imported so many items from Rome that it was called 'the kingdom of Roman culture'. Of course not all the artifacts are from Rome and there are many from Central Asia as well. The most representative Roman artifact is the glass dish that I covered in the introduction. These types of dishes are not found in neighboring countries like Baekje or Goguryeo. When importing foreign culture and institutions, Silla often did this through the more developed countries of Baekje and Goguryeo. But the riddle of how these items ended up in Silla without leaving any trace in Baekje or Goguryeo remains unsolved. Similar in style to glass artifacts found in southern Russia, the Mediterranean coast or western Asia, there is no doubt that there was some type of exchange going on between Silla and these areas.

One surprising point is that among the glass artifacts is a tall glass bottle that closely resembles the Oinokoe, a bottle used to store wine in the Mediterranean region. As I have just said, this shows that Silla was engaged in some type of trade with Rome. Also, Silla kings enjoyed wearing not only gold crowns but also gold earrings, necklaces, bracelets and lots of other accessories all at once; this is far from Chinese custom. Research shows that this was a style that was enjoyed by Roman nobility. Although I am not sure whether Silla aristocrats really were copying the fashion style of Rome, one

• •

'Smiling Jade' Necklace found in Daeneungwon
©Gyeongju National Meseum

thing that is certain is that this was not derived from China.

　　We can also see that there was definitely a connection between Silla and Rome by observing the 'smiling jade' necklace. This
necklace was also found in a tomb in Daeneungwon and is currently
displayed at Gyeongju National Museum. The glass beads of the
edge of this necklace are what draw our attention. Onto these tiny
beads that are not quite 1.8 centimeters[0.71 in] in diameter are carved
six people, six swans and two tree branches on the front and back.
The fact that so many finely done drawings were carved into this
small bead reflects the high level of technology that existed back

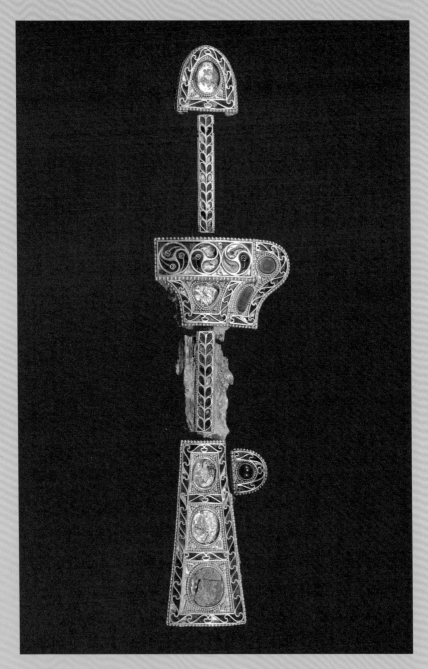

● ● The Sword found in Daeneungwon ©Gycongju National Meseum

then. But what is truly shocking here is that the faces are of Aryan Caucasians. Scholars hypothesize that these people were Central Asians living inside the Roman cultural sphere. Thus, it is clear that this necklace was made in Central Asia and imported into Silla. But strangely enough, similar artifacts were not found either in China or any other country. If these items had reached Silla via the Silk Road from Central Asia, they should be able to be found in the major cities along that route, but this is not the case.

One interesting sword was also found here at Daeneung-won. At a length of 36 centimeters(little over 1ft), it is highly ornate. It may not even seem like a sword. Perhaps this is why only a handful of similar swords have been found in the world. There are two main hypotheses about the origins of this sword: one states that it is a native Silla product while the other argues that it was imported from abroad. Whichever hypothesis is correct, scholars generally agree that the techniques used on this sword as well as the designs were clearly influenced by Greco-Roman culture. If you look at the surface of the sword, you will see that it is decorated with gold microbeads and jade; the spiral and medallion designs that are also used are typical Greco-Roman designs. The prevalent opinion is that the sword either came directly from Rome or it was crafted in a region that was influenced by Roman culture. The fact that this type of sword was not found in China but in the small country at the edge of it in Gyeongju is a true paradox. This is also displayed at Gyeongju National Museum.

The next strange artifact that we will see is similar. On first glance it is difficult to tell what it is but it was a wine glass. It is also called a horn glass because it is shaped like a horn. It is said that this glass was originally made out of animal horns and used by various nomadic tribes; it was then imported and adapted by Rome. Research shows that Romans imported this glass and decorated its edges with various elements of Greek legends like figures of women and animals. But the one you see here is not that fancy and is the relatively simple form that was used by nomadic people. As with the others, this glass too is not found in neighboring Baekje or Goguryeo but only the closest countries to Silla like Gaya, northern China

● ●

Clay Glass

and parts of Japan. It is still a mystery as to how this glass made it to Silla after skipping over Goguryeo and Baekje.

While we are on the subject of wine glasses, many artifacts are discovered in tombs in Daeneungwon as well as others in Silla and Gaya that are clay glasses with handles. These glasses too were influenced by Roman culture because similar examples are not found in Northeast Asian countries like China, Korea or Japan but are found in various European countries including Rome where the use of the handle had become firmly established. After seeing various Silla artifacts that prove that there was exchange between the European continent and Central Asia, you begin to reconsider the international nature of Silla culture.

● ●

Central Asian statue found in one of the tombs of Silla Kings

Before we move onto the next chapter, let's look at just a few more artifacts that show the extent of how cosmopolitan Silla culture was. It would not have been that difficult to encounter foreigners in Silla when it was at the height of its power in the mid-eighth century. We can make such educated guesses today because evidence of this is still constantly being discovered. As you can see in this picture, this stern-faced statue was found in front of the tomb of a Silla king. Judging from the clearly defined bicep muscles and the metal club in his hand, this person was probably a warrior who guarded the king's tomb. But you can tell from his deep-set eyes, large nose and thick beard that he is not Mongolian. This person is probably Indo-European or Turkish. Many people from these regions migrated to Silla and some of them worked as bodyguards for Silla nobility. The fact that they were carved on guardian statues of the king's tomb shows that they were not uncommon. Gyeongju was one of the four great ancient cities of the world partly due to this type of background.

There is one artifact that is always mentioned when discussing the cosmopolitan nature of Gyeongju. It is the 'Persian stone'. It is currently displayed in the front courtyard of Gyeongju National Museum, and was probably meant to be used to build a noble's house. If you look closely at the design, there is a tree at the center and a peacock on either side of it. The face of the peacock on the right is a lion while the one on the left is unfinished. All of these designs were popular in Persia[modern-day Iran] at that time. We can see just how much Silla was basking in cosmopolitanism in that these designs were decorating the houses of the nobility. To summarize what we have seen thus far, Silla culture consisted of a foundation of its own native culture with a combination of Chinese culture from the north, coastal culture from the south and Roman culture on top of all of this. Thus, the resulting culture was highly diverse and multidimensional.

This should be sufficient explanation about Silla tombs.

• •

'Persian Stone' in the front courtyard of
Gyeongju National Museum

Now it is time to go to Mount Nam, our next destination. There
are so many artifacts and historic sites at Mount Nam that the entire mountain has been registered with UNESCO. Although it is a
mountain, it will not take long to get there because it is close to the
downtown area.

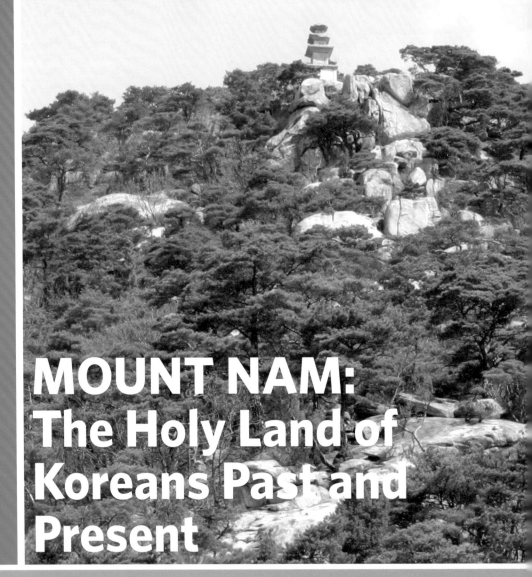

Chapter ❸

MOUNT NAM:
The Holy Land of
Koreans Past and
Present

Heading toward the western foot of Mount Nam

Scaling Mount Nam through Samneung Valley

In search of the Buddha statues

To the next valley: Yongjanggol

At the mention of Mount Nam, Koreans typically think of the one in Seoul. But because 'Mount Nam' is a common noun that simple means 'mountain in the south', Mount Nam is not found only in Seoul. From an international perspective, the Mount Nam in Gyeongju can be said to be more famous than its counterpart in Seoul. This is because as stated in the beginning, the former is registered as a UNESCO world heritage item. But Koreans are still not very familiar with the Mount Nam in Gyeongju although it is one of the city's most representative districts. Why else would Gyeongju natives say 'you have not visited Gyeongju if you have not climbed Mount Nam?'

Mount Nam is only a ten-minute drive from downtown Gyeongju. The mountain is called Mount Nam because it lies south of Wolseong, where the king lives(the Korean word 'nam' means 'south'). Thus, Mount Nam was a familiar place that people frequently visited during the Silla dynasty. At a height of not quite 500 meters[1,640ft], it is not a tall mountain in an absolute sense. But the countless tiny valleys, strangely-shaped stones and the pine tree forests at the foot of the mountain make it look much bigger than it actually is. The many Buddha statues and pagodas scattered throughout the mountain also create the impression of an outdoor museum. Before Buddhism entered Silla, people believed that this mountain was the home of the gods. After Buddhism entered, people seem to have changed their belief so that it was not gods but Buddha himself who inhabited Mount Nam. This is an entirely personal opinion, but it seems *probable considering the number of rock cliff Buddhas that are here. As the name suggests, a rock cliff Buddha is a Buddha image that has been carved into the surface of a rock. The image is carved in low relief not too deeply into the stone. This has the effect of making the Buddha look like it will walk right out of the stone. It is as if the carving was done so that the Buddha can step out of its stone framework to answer the fervent prayers of Buddhists. Because there are so many Buddha statues and pagodas all over the mountain, it is often called the holy land of Buddhists.*

There are currently 37 registered heritage items on Mount Nam. But this figure will probably increase in the future because more Buddha images continue to be discovered. Among the ones that were discovered later, there is one particular Buddha image that was very recently discovered hanging upside down as you can see in the photograph. It is not known exactly how long this Buddha was upside down, but there is no doubt that it is at least 1000 years old. The prevalence of countless other examples like this one is the reason why Mount Nam is known as both a holy land as well as an outdoor museum. But it would be a big mistake to think that the 37 artifacts registered at UNESCO are all that there is at Mount Nam. While 37 is not a small number, there used to be many more artifacts and relics on this mountain. It is said that there are over 150 temple sites that have been discovered; the number would be three times bigger if the still-buried sites were to be included. Also, there are said to be over 460 Buddha images and pagodas altogether. Included in this figure are ones that have been damaged beyond repair. The majority of the Buddhas found on Mount Nam are neither elegant nor graceful; most of them do not show any signs of fine craftsmanship. This is most likely because these are the works of lesser nobles who failed to form their own base in the capital city as well as commoners. That is why the Buddha statues and images found here look nothing like the perfection that is in Seokguram Grotto.

We must now climb up Mount Nam. There are various paths that are available to take. Because the relics are located here and there along various hiking trails, it is impossible to see them all within a day or two. There are some paths that have been created solely for the purpose of seeing a couple relics. The path leading to the Temple of Seven Buddhas is one example of this; this course takes a full day to complete. As you can see in the picture, the Temple of Seven Buddhas is a breathtakingly beautiful place. It is a recommended tour course because of the high quality of the Buddha statues, but it is not the right course for beginners. It is more beneficial for beginners to take paths that will expose them to the largest quantities of Buddhist relics and as much of Mount Nam as possible. Courses that fall into this latter category include the Three Tombs Valley(Samneung Valley) course. The name 'Three Tombs Valley' comes from the fact that three kings of Later Silla are believed to be buried at the foot of the mountain. It is not that arduous of a hike, but the best part is that many artifacts and relics can be seen. Because it takes approximately 3~4 hours to go and come back, the entire course can be completed in just half a day.

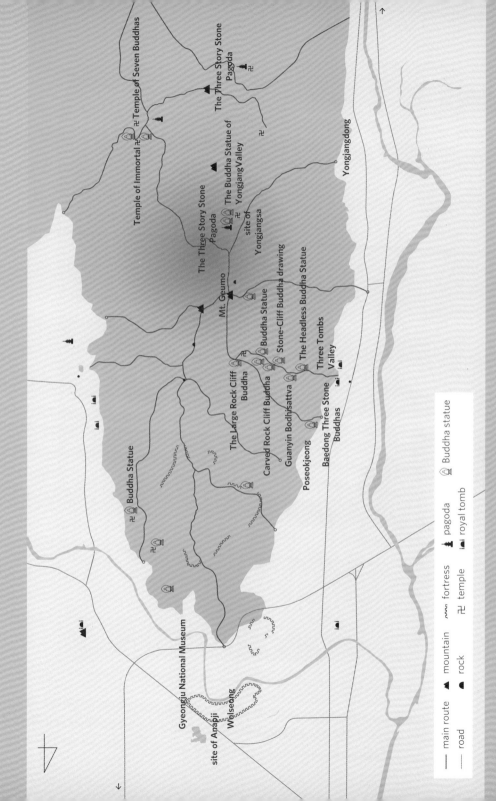

Temple of Immortal 卍 Temple of Seven Buddhas

The Three Story Stone Pagoda

The Three Story Stone Pagoda

The Buddha Statue of Yongjang Valley 卍 Yongjang Valley

site of Yongjangsa

Yongjiangdong

Mt. Geumo

Stone-Cliff Buddha drawing

Buddha Statue

The Headless Buddha Statue

The Large Rock Cliff Buddha

Three Tombs Valley

Carved Rock Cliff Buddha

Guanyin Bodhisattva

Poseokjeong

Baedong Three Stone Buddhas

Buddha Statue

Gyeongju National Museum

Wolseong

site of Anapji

—— main route	▲ mountain	⛩ Buddha statue
—— road	◆ rock	
ᨫ fortress	卍 temple	▲ pagoda
		⚱ royal tomb

• • Map of Mount Nam

● ● Buddha Statues of the Temple of Seven Buddhas

Heading toward the western foot of Mount Nam

The place that we will visit first here at the western foot of the mountain is a place called Najeong. Najeong is the name of the pond that used to be here. At a glance, there is not much to see because there is only a small house. The significance of this site is found in the legend that is connected to this spot. It is famous because it is where the first king of Silla, Park Hyeokgeose, was 'discovered'. Because the nation of Silla had not yet been formed at this time, it is more accurate to use the name Gyeongju. There were six tribal chiefs in the Gyeongju region at that time, and it seems that a powerful outsider tribe entered itself into the mix. The chief of this outsider tribe was eventually crowned as king and this was Park Hyeokgeose. This is how the story is told by later generations: The six tribal chiefs had a meeting to decide upon a virtuous candidate to be crowned king. While they were meeting, they saw a strange energy sweep through Najeong and then one white horse that sat bowing before something. When the chiefs arrived on the scene they found that the horse had brought an egg. The horse then cried at length before ascending back to the heavens. Inside the egg was a tidy-looking boy, who after being raised for ten years was crowned king in 57 BC.

There are many interpretations of this legend; while we cannot go through all of them here, let's go over the one that seems to make the most sense. The legend states that a horse brought an egg: this can be seen as the coming of the northern nomadic tribes because the horse is an essential aspect of nomadic culture. On the other hand, the egg is seen as a symbol of southern culture. Thus, the horse bringing an egg can be interpreted as the mixing of people from the northern and southern areas. Here, the northern people are foreigners while the southern people are natives of the area; the former conquered the latter and made themselves king. Park Hyeokgeose symbolizes the leader of this foreign tribe. However, even these Park family kings are eventually pushed out of power by the newcomer Kim clan. Regardless of what happened afterwards, this is a highly important site because it was the origin of the Park lineage, one of the most common last names in Korea.

If you walk less than a mile after reaching the main road from Najeong, you will see a signboard that reads 'Poseokjeong'. This is where the king of Silla and his officials would come to have a good time by floating their drinking glasses on the water. Today the entire site looks rather creepy because it has not been properly cared for, but it probably looked much fancier in its day. As you can see in the picture, a small artificial stream was created with stone on which glasses were floated around. This artificial device was designed so that when the glass had traveled a certain distance, it would stop and then spin in place. Then, the person sitting there would have to either create a poem on the spot or drink what was inside the glass. It may sound simple enough, but it is actually extremely difficult to construct a device that does this. It requires highly advanced hydrostatic calculations as well as hundreds of trial-and-error attempts. But looking at it today, it does not seem to be a very sophisticated structure at all. This is probably because it has been more or less abandoned to the elements. The reason that it has not been properly renovated probably is connected to its sad history. The penultimate king of Silla was attacked by enemy forces while enjoying a par-

• •
Poseokjeong

ty here. The king was forced to commit suicide and the queen was raped: in short, it was truly an unspeakable tragedy. Perhaps later generations have chosen to leave this place alone because of the humiliating past that is represented by it.

If you walk half a mile onto the main road from here, you will come across a signboard that reads 'Three Stone Buddhas^{Samjonbul}'. Technically, the correct name is 'Baedong Three Stone Buddhas' because Baedong is the name of this area. This Buddha statue is another one that absolutely must be seen when you visit Mount Nam. As with the relics that we have just seen, it is located not too far inward from the main road and so is a timesaver. You do not even have to worry about parking because there are nice parking facilities here. You can see at a glance that this is very much a Korean-style statue. I have not seen that many Chinese and Japanese Buddha statues, but to date I have not yet seen a Buddha in either of these countries that looks as genial as these three. The faces of Buddha statues are said to resemble those of the people living in that area; Silla people must have looked like this. While the expression is appropriately elegant, it is at the same time very approachable and looks almost friendly. One interesting feature of these three Buddha figures is the smile on the face of the middle Buddha. The body is of an adult but the face has the sweet innocence of a smiling child. The people of Silla apparently did not see Buddha as a forbidding figure but one who could

226

GYEONGJU, The Heart of Korean Culture

easily be befriended. The statues here look very different from the dignified expression on the Buddha inside Seokguram Grotto.

This may be an entirely personal opinion, but I believe that this embodies everything that makes a Korean sculpture. There are many features of Korean aesthetics, one of them being this type of kindly and down-to-earth appearance. From the perspective of Koreans, traditional Japanese art looks too uptight while those of China depict human beings in too positive of a light. Koreans, as in the face of this Buddha, argue that this type of comfortable aura is seen often in Korean art. There is no need to think anything else while looking at this Buddha. All you need to do is to assume the same facial expression as that of this Buddha. A similar type of Buddha statue can be found at the Gyeongju National Museum. The face of the Buddha at the museum is so animated and childish that it is called the 'Baby Buddha'. As you can see in the picture(p.283), the face of this Buddha looks exactly like that of a baby. We will come back to this statue when we reach the museum.

Despite my praise for this Buddha, its face unfortunately cannot be seen if you visit this site. These three Buddhas were actually separate statues that were gathered from different locations to this spot. Because of this, there did not used to be a roof here and you could view them by sunlight. This allowed you to clearly see each face. However, it is no longer possible to properly view these Buddhas because of the roof that was built over them in the name of artifact protection. It is difficult to see them because of the shadow created on the inside. That beautiful smile is no longer visible. Instead, all that are in its place are some candles and offerings laid out by Buddhists in worship. The ignorance of later generations has ruined yet another opportunity to view a beautiful artifact. While renovation technology of Korean has improved, it still has a long way to go in terms of paying attention to the details. All we can do is wait for more time to go by.

Scaling Mount Nam through Samneung Valley

After leaving Baedong and walking another half mile or so, you will come to an entrance. Called Samneung(Three Tombs) Valley, this is the course that we will take to hike up Mount Nam. I first came here in the early 1990s. Because this was before Mount Nam became known, there were not a lot of people around. It was a time when people automatically thought of the mountain in Seoul when asked about Mount Nam and practically nobody knew about the one in Gyeongju. The parking lot was not large because of the dearth of visitors. It was that quiet of a place back then. But now there is a parking lot just across the street that can accommodate many cars. While it is good that more people are interested in this place, it also means that cultural heritages will suffer more damage because of the high degree of traffic. This concerns me each time I visit Mount Nam. Ever since the larger parking lot was built, I have greatly missed the quiet calm of Mount Nam that is such a stark contrast to the bustling chaos that is here today. I guess it is impossible to avoid becoming a blind supporter of the past the more field trips that I take.

After parking and crossing the road to the entrance, there is an information board. It always helps to look over this type of information board and the map included on it before going to see

229

the actual site because it helps your understanding of it. When you arrive at a historic site, do not start immediately moving around but first take a moment to observe the information board. One particularly important feature of these boards is the map that shows you at a glance what there is to see and where. The place that we will be heading toward is the top of this valley. We can also know that there are six historic sites — albeit all to do with Buddhism — along the way. Apart from the Buddhist sites there are also a few other things to see, and nowhere else in all of Mount Nam are there so many historic sites grouped together in one valley. I highly recommend this valley to beginners because it allows you to see both historic relics as well as Mount Nam. One point to keep in mind before starting on the tour is that although Mount Nam is not an extremely tall mountain high, it is not that easy to climb. Also, because in most cases you are not only simply hiking up the mountain but also going to various historic sites in between the path is a rather difficult one. Ancient people did not only sculpt Buddha statues in convenient and easily-reached places but also at very high locations that would be pleasing to the eye as seen from below.

With these facts in mind, let's be on our way up the mountain. The first thing that you will see is a field of pine trees. The pine trees here are actually quite reputable. It is interesting that the Mount Nam in Seoul is also well-known for its pine trees. The defining

Pine Trees in Mount Nam

• •
Bent Crossbeams of
a Buddhist Temple

characteristic of the Korean pine tree is its twisted and bent form. Koreans loved pine trees that were as bent over as possible and gave them the highest grade. We can see this same philosophy in works of art as well. Koreans in the past liked to use curved lines rather than straight lines in art. There are countless examples that I could name, but let's discuss only the most representative one here. In this piece, you will see in a glance how much Koreans loved curved lines. The picture that you see is of the pillar and crossbeam of a Buddhist temple building. Koreans at the time preferred to use bent and twisted trees for the pillar even though trees with straight trunks were also available. In other words, this tree was not used because straight ones were unavailable but because the architect believed that the bent tree was better suited for the aesthetics of the building. Of these two photos, the one with the bent tree looks so extreme that it looks like it was altered with computer graphics. The proof that this selection was a matter of choice and not necessity is in the inner part of this building: all of the pillars there are made of straight trees.

I think that Koreans have an affinity for bent trees because of these circumstances. But the pine trees here are not very old ones because as you can see, they are not large. Most of them are less than 100 years old, but the ones that Koreans love are usually much older and much more bent than these. These trees are often photographed by professional photographers. There is an eminent Korean photographer who often took pictures of these kinds of pine trees and they are worth tens of millions of won. If you climb a little past this pine tree forest you will see three hills. But these are not really hills but tombs of Silla kings. Because there are three tombs, this valley is called 'Three Tomb Valley ^{Samneung gyegok}'.

In search of the Buddha statues

There is not much time to spend at these tombs because we still have a long way to go. A ten minute walk from here will lead to the first artifact. It is a headless Buddha statue. Not only does it not have a head but it does not have hands either, meaning that the statue most likely rolled off from where it used to be. This statue was found at the valley below this and moved to where it stands today. Thus, no one is sure of its original location. For reasons unknown, this Buddha statue was hurled to the bottom of the valley and is now a handicapped Buddha. Although it has been severely damaged, we

• • The Headless Buddha Statue

can see the finely sculpted lines in what is left of it and that it was thus not a careless creation. Perhaps this is why although it may be a handicapped Buddha, you can always see people worshipping at this statue. Whenever I visit here, I can see a lit candle and a few small offerings in front of the statue. The most obvious proof of the fine craftsmanship can be seen in the knot right below the left shoulder. The knot has been so finely carved out that while looking at it you almost forget the fact that it is made of stone. But this Buddha statue is dressed differently from other Buddhas. It looks as if it is wearing the robes of a monk. It is rare for a Buddha statue to be wearing this type of attire. This is why there are those who argue that this is actually a monk statue, but I do not think this is likely.

Because there are so many missing parts, there is not much more to see of this statue. Let us now leave it behind and look for other relics. Another relic appears once you have gone up the sloping path to the left of the Buddha. It does not seem like anything would be there, but this is the way it is for all of Mount Nam. Relics are found in completely unlikely places and thus are difficult to find without guidance. I remember when I first visited Mount Nam twenty years ago that I kept my eyes wide searching every rock that I saw, not wanting to miss anything that may have been carved on it. Of course, I did not find anything myself. This is why the categorization of relics on Mount Nam is a work in progress. We do not know what kind of relic is hiding where.

If you go up the sloping path on the left-hand side, you will see a Buddha statue through the branches of the pine trees. It is actually not a Buddha but a statue of a bodhisattva. I will not explain the term 'bodhisattva' here because I have already done so at length at Seokguram Grotto. Instead, let's go over the differences between a Buddha statue and a bodhisattva statue. Temples are full of Buddha statues, but there are so many types of these that they are not easily distinguishable to a beginner. Even among Buddha statues there are many types, including Śākyamuni Buddha, Amitabha Buddha, Medicine Buddha, Vairocana Buddha, etc, but these have some characteristics in common. One such characteristic is that they do not wear anything on their heads. However, a bodhisattva always has crown-like headgear. Very simply speaking, any statue with no crown is a Buddha and any statue with a crown is a bodhisattva. Here, a bodhisattva is like an assistant of the Buddhas. The rough equivalent in Christianity is an angel.

I have said that bodhisattvas always wear crowns, but there is one exception. If you see a Buddha statue that does not wear a crown and has green hair, it is a bodhisattva named Ksitigarbha. Ksitigarbha is in charge of hell and is said to be extremely busy saving the souls that are there. He has stated that he will not leave as long as there is even one sinful soul in hell; if this is true, it does not look like he can leave anytime soon. This is obviously because as saved ones leave hell, more enter from the living world to take their places. But I am not sure why Ksitigarbha does not wear a crown and has green hair.

Ksitigarbha Bodhisattva

In the midst of such thoughts we have already arrived at a Buddha^{Guanyin Bodhisattva} statue. The path to it is a very short one. The rock on which this Buddha has been carved is a relatively long one. A rock that would not have had any value by itself is now a holy rock because a Buddha has been carved onto it. We can still see the Buddha, but can also see that the image has become greatly faded because so many years have passed. Thus, although we do not know exactly what it originally looked like, we can see that it was not a low-grade sculpture because of the dignified aura that it radiates. When looking at the rock cliff Buddhas at Mount Nam, there are many cases in which the upper part is carved in high relief and the lower part looks rather blurred. Why were they carved in this way? There are various theories, but the one that I find most convincing is that the Buddha statues are carved in this way to portray the Buddha as if he has just emerged from the rock.

To think about this more broadly, the people of Silla believed that the entirety of Mount Nam was equal to the body of Buddha. Thus, they believed that if they prayed hard enough, the Buddha inside the rock would come out and save them. Similarly, the statue that we have just seen has emerged from the rock in answer to the people's prayers. But this statue is interpreted slightly differently from the others. It can be seen as emerging from the rock or as having come down from heaven. This hypothesis is a convincing one because of the amount of rock that there is above the bodhisattva image. It is said that the long length of rock is the distance that Guanyin came down. This explanation sounded highly probable when I first heard it, and it seems even more so the more I think about it. But depending on different views, the rock behind it

● ●

Guanyin Bodhisattva ©Guseok Kim

can seem like a halo. For these kinds of explanations, it is impossible to point to any one as the correct theory because they all seem likely.

If you look carefully at this statue, you will see that its right hand is upon its breast and its left hand is holding a bottle. The hand on its breast is probably a portrayal of the giving of a sermon. The bottle in the left hand most likely contains clean water. One of the duties of a bodhisattva is curing the sick. A bodhisattva can cure illness with medicine but also with clean water. Clean water had curative powers in India because the water was dirty in general. This bodhisattva is gradually revealing herself to this world already prepared to cure the sick. But if you look at this statue, you will see a slight reddish tinge on the lips. This is because this portion of the rock was originally red; the attention to detail that planned out the statue so that the lips would be right at this part is astounding. Because this statue is also a well-made one, it would be in your best interest to observe it carefully by looking all around it.

In order to go to the next relic we must return to the Buddha statue below. After hiking just a few minutes after having reached the bottom again, you will see a large rock on which a picture has been carved. A close look will show that these lines draw a Buddha image. This rock is divided into roughly two parts: on one part are three Buddhas. These Buddhas are usually called 'stone cliff Buddha drawings' because, made up of only lines, they are closer to

Stone-Cliff Buddha drawing(left part) ©Guseok Kim

drawings than statues. Thus, this along with the drawing of the flying horse that we saw at Daeneungwon is considered the only surviving drawing from the Silla dynasty. The lines near the top of the rock are not very clear because of age, but there is no difficulty in grasping the general layout of the picture. You will see that in the middle of each rock is a Buddha with bodhisattvas on either side of it. But in the picture on the left, the Buddha is standing while the bodhisattva is in a sitting position while presenting him with something. In the picture on the right, the Buddha is sitting on a lotus flower while the bodisattvas are standing.

When seeing these Buddha statues, there is always the question of which Buddha is being portrayed, but there is no definite answer. According to my guess, the left represents the west and so the Buddha depicted here is Amitabha Buddha. Thus, the Buddha on the right is Śākyamuni Buddha. The reason why the Buddha on the left is assumed to be Amitabha Buddha is that paradise, the heaven of Buddhism, is 'Western Pure Land' or the pure land to the west. Having Amitabha and Śākyamuni Buddha together in one place is an old tradition in Buddhism. Have we not seen the same phenomenon at Bulguksa? Buddhists worship Śākyamuni while they are alive and then go to paradise where Amitabha Buddha is after death. In this way, life before and after death is fully accounted for and there is nothing more to fear in life. The fervent prayers of the Silla people can be felt here at Mount Nam as well.

The key point that we should take away from this work of art is not anything to do with Buddhist doctrine but the lines of the drawing. It may not seem important on first glance, but the power of these lines is anything but ordinary. We must not forget that these drawings have been done on rock. Remember that these clear and flowing lines were made onto granite. The fact that the lines are not deep in some places and shallow in others and are instead of uniform depth throughout is an amazing one. It would not have been an easy task. Without a combination of technical skill and artistic vision, a work such as this would have been impossible.

To go to the next relic, go up the path to the left when facing this drawing. Once you have thus climbed to the top of the rock on which this drawing has been done, you will find that there is a straight gash. This is to prevent rainwater from flowing down onto the drawing. Rainwater flowing onto the drawing would have caused it to gradually blur as well as assist the formation of moss and other substances; this was foreseen and prevented. We can see the desire to protect their object of worship. There are also two holes into which pillars can be placed on either side of the gash. Four pillars would have been used to support a roof over the rock, and religious ceremonies would have been held under it. We can tell that there was indeed a roof here because of the various bits of roof tiles that have been found on this spot. Even today roof tile fragments are found on the ground, but these are from the Silla dynasty that was 1000 years ago. It is unfortunate that this site has not been renovated properly; I cannot help thinking that it would have looked a lot better with the roof in place.

Let's now climb a little higher. There did not used to be a path here but it was created by the many people who came here to look at the Buddha statue above. I remember wondering why people were going where there was no path when I first visited here 20 years ago. If you go up a steep hell, you will see a rock cliff Buddha like the one in the picture. This Buddha has been carved on a rock approximately 10 meters [33ft] high; what is interesting here is that as shown in the photo, the Buddha was carved onto the rock even though it was a crevice in the middle. One might think that it is unnecessary to carve on a cracked rock, but the point was to use the natural surroundings exactly the way it is. I personally believe that this attempt to leave nature as untouched as possible reflects

Carved Rock Cliff Buddha

the aesthetic sensibility of Koreans. But this itself may be an over-interpretation because the person who carved this Buddha probably did so without much thought.

The unique feature of this Buddha statue is the fact that its face is in bas relief but the rest of the body is drawn using lines. Something about the face, however, looks rather awkward. The lips and nose are too thick and the overall composition of the face does not look natural. Compared to the Buddhas that we have seen thus far, this one is clearly a little below par. I am not completely sure, but it seems that the person who carved this Buddha was not artistically inclined. This opens it to the hypothesis that this person was not a member of a high social class. When sculpting, it is best not to do the face in bas relief. This is because it is not an easy task to carve a three-dimensional face on a flat rock surface. While there would have been no problems had the face been done with lines, it seems that the person who sculpted this Buddha ended up creating facial features that are far from beautiful in his efforts to create a three-dimensional face. Nonetheless, we can see that the other parts that have been drawn with lines actually look fairly nice. We can conclude that the artist was proficient with lines but not at three-dimensional sculpture. It may also have been that the person who sponsored this artist somehow ran out of funds to pay him with in the end and that is why the sculpture is unfinished. Still, this Buddha remains popular because the hands have been beautifully sculpted.

Our next destination can be reached if you go just a little father below this Buddha statue. The paths here are difficult to follow without guidance. Also, they are not very optimal for walking so you must be careful. The sitting Buddha that we will now see used to be here in its damaged state until just recently. When I visited in 2008, I was not able to see the Buddha at all because it was being renovated. Had it not been damaged, it may have been the best Buddha statue in all of Mount Nam. But a look at the face before renovation shows that it was in critical condition. The part below the eyes had been clumsily filled in with cement. The reason for this is that construction workers who were fixing this statue during the Japanese colonial period simply pasted it over with cement. I remember that whenever we took field trips here, we would cover up the disgraceful looking bottom part of the face with a piece of cloth. Once that part was covered, we would exclaim at the beauty of the eyes and forehead of this Buddha because it was similar to the elegance of Seokguram Grotto. I remember laughing at the face after we removed the cloth because the face suddenly changed from that of a beautiful Buddha to a stupid and vacant expression.

Also, the halo was found behind the Buddha statue broken into pieces. The halo was in its original position even up to the 1960s. However, it is said that an intoxicated passerby smashed it

Buddha Statues before and after renovation
©Guseok Kim

to pieces. I can not help wondering why anyone would drink all the way over here, and even if the person was drunk there was no need to have disturbed a cultural relic. At that time, annual per capita income in Korea was only a few hundred dollars; at a point at which cultural awareness had hit rock-bottom, accidents like this would not have been unheard of. However, all of this is in the past. The statue has now been fully restored as you can see in the photo. The face has been renovated and the halo is back up as well. With its round and plump body, this Buddha has the most prodigious carriage out of all the Buddhas near this vlley. The reason for its relative obesity is most likely that Silla was at its peak when it was built. Because the nation was well-off, the Buddha was also sculpted to look fat and bountiful.

In terms of renovation, there is nothing else problematic about this Buddha statue. However, if there is a problem it has to do with the face, the most sensitive and difficult portion. On the face, even a 1 mm difference is enough to create vast differences in appearance. While it looks like the renovations on the face have been done well, I still get the impression that the face looks a little fat. However, I cannot make any definitive comments on this because we do not know exactly what it originally looked like. The right cheek is especially awkward. The excessive protruding of the right cheek throws off the balance of the entire face and makes it look strange.

The shortness of the neck also seems to affect the facial proportions; because the experts who were in charge argue that that was the original appearance of the statue, it looks like we regular people have nothing to say to that. Another question that forms in my mind about this statue is why such a good-quality statue was created so deep in the mountains. Because this is not an open area, there would not only have been a Buddha statue. There was a temple here as well. Although it has not been rebuilt yet, the site has been found right next to the statue.

We have now seen all of the relics in the middle area of Mount Nam. Now let's head toward the top of the mountain. If you walk a little towards the top after having passed by a small temple in between, there is a large rock to the left and a fairly large empty lot in front of it. This rock is over 6 meters^{almost 20ft} tall and on it is carved a large Buddha. It has been done in a similar method as the other Buddhas that we have seen. The head and upper part of the body have been sculpted in relief so that it protrudes outward while the rest has been drawn with lines. As with the Buddhas we have already seen, this can be interpreted as the Buddha gradually coming out of the rock. If we think about the motive of the people who created this, would they not have wanted the Buddha sleeping inside the rock to come out to answer their fervent prayers? Thus, the Buddha has begun emerging from the head portion and the rest of the body

The Large Rock Cliff Buddha ©Guseok Kim

has not yet come out.

I personally like this Buddha statue very much. The technical skill is good but what I like most is its location. Because it is almost at the top of the mountain, the view below from the empty lot in front of it is breathtaking. The people of Silla probably chose this location on purpose for its view. While they busily live their lives below, they wanted this Buddha to always be looking out for them. Perhaps this is why the face is bent slightly downward. It seems that he is listening to all of our prayers and wishes even now. This cannot be seen very well from right in front of the statue. If you climb a little higher up the mountain and look at the statue from the ridgeline across from here, you will be able to see that the head is slightly bent over. It is a wonderful sight when directly in front of the statue, but its real beauty comes out when viewing it from the opposite ridgeline as shown in the photo.

In addition, the large empty lot is a good place to worship in front of the statue. This indicates that it was loved from the Silla dynasty all the way up to the present-day. Perhaps it is for this reason that recently(in 2009) a famous drama set in the Silla dynasty was filmed here. Each time I visit I feel that this should be designated as a National Treasure, but this will probably not happen anytime soon. This Buddha statue is not a treasure of the nation but merely a designated cultural artifact of this province. Not only does this statue have huge artistic and religious significance but it is also over 1000 years old; these conditions would make it easy to be designated as a National Treasure, but apparently experts do not share this opinion. Whatever the situation may be, the wide area where you can take a rest is the perfect place to spend time and fully enjoy this beautiful statue.

To the next valley: Yongjanggol

This finishes up all of the Buddha statues in this valley. To go to our next destination, we must climb a little higher from where we are to another valley called Yongjanggol(Yongjang Valley) but the path is not an easy one. Those who are tired at this point should return back down the mountain by the same path taken up here. The area surrounding Yongjang Valley is short but is quite difficult, requiring that you hold onto a rope for part of the way. Let's now take the Mount Nam Beltway in search of Yongjang Valley. This path was created in case of forest fires, so it was built wide enough for a car to pass through. After a little while, you will come to a fork in the road: the left will take you to the Temple of Seven Buddhas and the right leads to Yongjang Valley. We are of course going to Yongjang Valley

• • The Stone Pagoda of Yongjang Valley

but it is a pity that we cannot visit the Temple of Seven Buddhas as there are many beautiful Buddha statues there that are considered treasures.

Let's turn toward Yongjang Valley. Not long after passing the fork in the road, we can see one lonely pagoda. It is the famous stone pagoda of Yongjangsa. It was not made to be viewed from above as shown in the picture. On first glance it looks so ordinary that you may wonder why it was built here at all. Only 4.5 meters[14.8ft] high, it does not inspire much awe. The secret lies in the view upward from the bottom of the valley. If you look back on it while walking down the valley, the pagoda looks taller and more dignified the further down the valley you go. Even from far away, the clear outline of the pagoda that greets the eye never ceases to amaze visitors. As it is too difficult to explain this phenomenon in words, we will have to make do with this picture.

This pagoda was designed with this purpose in mind. In other words, the pagoda was designed so that it could be seen from anywhere within this valley. Surprisingly, it was created according to Buddhist doctrine that it is at the center of the world. Thus it was built to be seen from anywhere. But don't you feel that you have seen this pagoda before? That's right! Does it not resemble Seokgatap that we saw earlier at Bulguksa? The only difference with this pagoda is that it is slightly smaller than Seokgatap. As I said earlier, most Korean pagodas built after Seokgatap were built modeled after Seokgatap. This shows once again that Seokgatap is the best of Korean pagodas.

A massive theoretical discussion about the worldview of Buddhism is usually always included in an explanation of this pagoda; for convenience's sake we will skip this. Instead I will only mention that this pagoda does not have its own foundation but uses the entire mountain as its foundation. A pagoda has many meanings including that of being Buddha's tomb. We must also keep in mind that the pagoda had a central role as a bridge connecting this world with the land of Buddha. The pagoda is a highly symbolic structure in which each floor beginning with its foundation stone are all seen as layers of heaven. As you climb each floor you are reaching closer to the Buddhist world, the focal point of the universe. Thus, we can go to the land of Buddha through the pagoda.

The foundation of the pagoda was originally meant to symbolize Mount Sumi, the mountain in the middle of the Buddhist world. This particular pagoda was built on the mountain itself instead of a separate foundation stone, making Mount Nam its foundation. Because of this, the bottom layer of this pagoda gives the impression of being unfinished unlike other pagodas. But this is not due to a lack of artistic sense but because of the effort to make this mountain the foundation. In this way, this world is connected to the

• • The Buddha Statue of Yongjang Valley

land of Buddha. Through this pagoda, we can see just how much the people of Silla wished to connect to heaven, the origin of all things.

The path that leads to our next destination is a bit rough but fortunately a short one. If you go just a little farther from this pagoda, you will encounter a Buddha statue unlike the ones that you have seen thus far. The fact that it does not have a neck is similar to various other Buddha statues in different valleys all over Mount Nam. But as you can see in the photo, the pedestal is highly unique. There are three tire-like objects stacked on top of each other and a drum-like object in between. Students who see this for the first time delightedly point out that it looks like three stacked hamburgers before even hearing my explanation. I could see why this explanation would be a lot more relatable to young people today! These three floors are slightly different in shape and size, but I will skip the rationale behind this because it would be too lengthy. I will only note that there are almost no Buddha statues in Korea that have round pedestals like this one. The fact that it is composed of three stories is an added novelty. Scholars are not sure of why this is, and so I also will not attempt to clear up this matter.

If you look at this pedestal, you will see that the bottom part is connected to the rock surface of the mountain beneath it. We have already seen this style in the pagoda that we just left behind. From the perspective of Buddhist doctrine, the incorporation of the stone surface indicates that the entire mountain symbolizes this world and each of the three circular stones represents one heaven in the Buddhist universe. Thus, the uppermost part where Maitreya Buddha resides symbolizes heaven; this is conveyed by making the pedestal on which Buddha is sitting a beautiful lotus flower. The highest heaven is decorated with lotus flowers. Along these lines, the lines of the cloth that flow down the pedestal are highly refined. It has been sculpted to look more elegant than actual clothing. The clothing of the Buddha statue itself has also been finely sculpted. The knot that looks exactly the way it does in real life is a particularly nice point.

Looking at the entire statue from this perspective, we can see that the bottom part makes use of nature while progressively more human touch is applied to the statue going up to result in the height of artificial beauty at the apex. In other words, nature and humans coexist within this Buddha statue. It is a definitive example of the aesthetic ideal that Koreans have traditionally supported.

This place contains not only this statue but also a rock cliff Buddha carved onto a stone directly behind it. The skill that carved this Buddha was a formidable one; the overall impression is clearly a refined one. According to scholars, this Buddha combines both dignity and compassion. You can feel the solemn dignity in the sharp bridge of the nose and the firmly closed lips and compassion in the fullness of the face and the soft outline of the chin. But the most no-

table feature of this Buddha is the many folds in the clothing. Compared to other Buddhas, for a reason unknown it has a lot more folds in its clothing. There is some writing next to the Buddha; it is not very clear but reads that the statue was created sometime in the late tenth or early eleventh century. It was not created during the Silla dynasty like the other relics but in the subsequent Goryeo dynasty.

We have now seen just about all the relics that there are to see at Yongjang Valley. Now the only task that awaits us is the trip back down the mountain. We have quite a long way to go because we are at the middle of the mountain. The road is also a difficult one. One comfort in this situation is that you can make it all the way down by continuously looking up at the pagoda. As you go down the mountain, the pagoda looks progressively smaller but also more dignified as it reduces in size. Because of this, it feels like this pagoda is a mystical place. These pictures have been taken, but it is difficult to capture the on-site atmosphere via camera. Once you have continued down for a while, you can no longer see the pagoda and the path becomes flat again.When you have come back down in this way you will see a village. It will be three or four in the afternoon by the time you have reached the main road. Because you would have begun around nine in the morning, the trip has basically taken all day. In some senses we have covered a lot today, but it is not a lot compared to all of the known relics on Mount Nam. At this point, it is a little too late to visit another site but still too early to call it a day for a field trip. But there is still one last place to visit and that is the Gyeongju National Museum, another treasure chest of Silla culture. The museum is not registered at UNESCO but it should be visited on any tour of Gyeongju because of the various priceless treasures that are preserved here. Not stopping by the museum in Gyeongju would be committing another word contradiction.

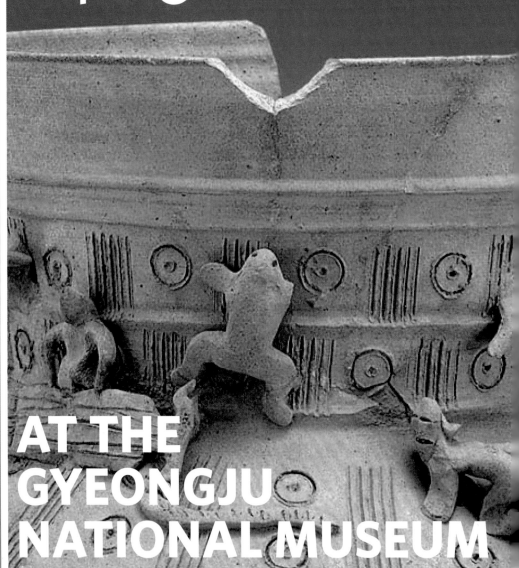

AT THE GYEONGJU NATIONAL MUSEUM

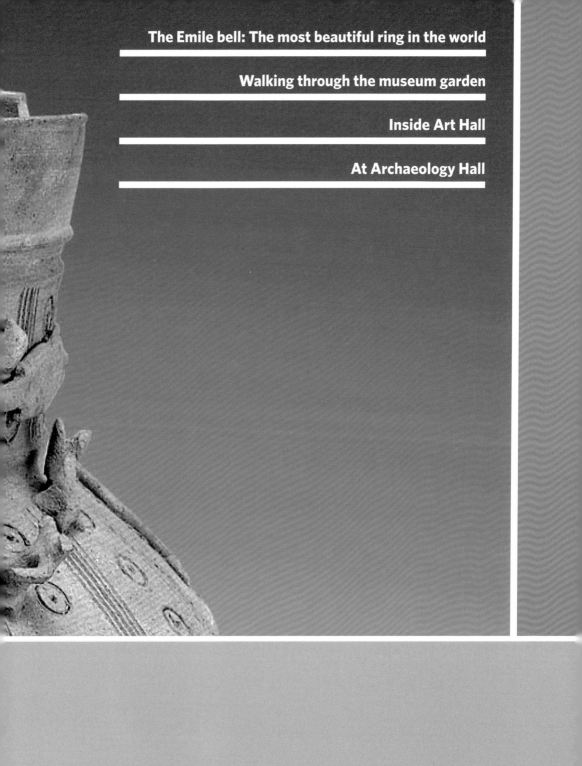

close to Daeneungwon and Anapji. There are many reasons why it is es-
sential to stop by here, but would not the most important one be the origi-
nal Emile bell? There are many stories that describe this bell, but they can
all be summarized in the phrase 'the bell that has the most beautiful ring
in the world.' You have no choice but to have this bell be the first thing you
see because it is displayed in the courtyard of the museum; let us also head
to this first. There are many more artifacts at the museum that are repre-
sentative objects of Silla culture. There are Buddha statues, firm pagodas,
sarira found inside these pagodas and other related items and even fun
artifacts like the clay figurines. There is also a separate exhibition hall that
displays the relics found in Anapji. We cannot see all of them but will go
through a few of the more representative items.

The Emile bell:
The most beautiful ring in the world

What can we possibly say about this bell? What can really
be said about this bell? Before you can say anything chances are that
you will forget it entirely. You will be left speechless because of the
mere fact that you are standing in front of this bell. The first thought
of visitors who see this bell should be amazement that a bell this

old still exists; the second should be gratitude. This bell was built in the mid-eighth century and thus has an extremely long past of 1200 years. Can there be a reason other than providence that it has survived intact through countless wars and the throes of history?

This bell was probably preserved by a temple during Silla and Goryeo because Buddhism was the state religion for both nations. But when the state religion was changed to Confucianism in the Joseon dynasty, it was thrown out into the grass fields where children would beat on it for fun and oxen would rub their horns on it. In other words, the bell was completely abandoned. This was most likely the result of government indifference due to the persecution of Buddhism at that time. The Confucian officials back then probably had no idea of the significance of this bell in world history. It was seen merely an object of the outsider religion[Buddhism] and left to its own devices. You can see in the picture that there are many headless Buddha statues in the back garden of the museum; this was the doing of Confucian intellectuals of the Joseon dynasty. If nothing was thought of decapitating the holiest object of Buddhist worship, it is not surprising that this bell had no significance. This abandoned bell was eventually moved next to the main gate of Gyeongju to ring at the opening and closing of the gate. To Joseon officials, this bell had no value apart from its most basic function. This bell was moved to a museum five years after the start of the Japanese colonial period in

● ● The Emile Bell

1915. It was then that the bell finally found its home. Having come to stand in the museum courtyard after such a long and arduous journey, it is no wonder that it is called a miracle of heaven. After the creation of this bell, Korea endured the invasions of Mongolia, Japan and the Jürchens, was colonized by Japan for about 40 years and then recently endured the Korean War. The bell survived all of these turbulent times, inviting the expression of heaven's aid.

What is even stranger is that it has sounded for 1200 years and still makes the most beautiful sound in the world. But most people who see this bell do not seem to think that it is so odd. But how is it that a 1200 year old object can still fulfill its function? Also, because a bell is continuously beaten, there is no knowing when it will crack. This is why it is so amazing that it has survived in one piece to this day without needing repair. If a crack forms on the surface or a piece breaks off altogether, it is extremely difficult to repair; considering this we can conclude that there have been no problems since its construction. It is impossible to not wonder how this bell could have lasted in perfect condition for over a century. It is the luxury good of luxury goods. It was hit 33 times exactly once a year on December 31st until the early 1980s. It is not beaten anymore for preservation purposes. It is unfortunate but said to be necessary for the continued preservation of the bell. This type of approach seems to be typical of a museum, which is always more interested in the preservation rather than functionality of a relic.

This bell not only has a beautiful ring but looks beautiful as well. Even those who see it for the first time immediately sense that the shape is very well-balanced proportionally. The angels that are carved into the bell's surface are also a sight to see. This method of depicting angels is typical Buddhist style, and these are considered some of the most beautiful. It is interesting that Buddhist angels are not winged like angels in the west but appear on cloud-like objects. This is to show that they are flying through the skies. There are four such angels on the bell and in between them are sections of writing that explains the process of how the bell was built and the names of people who participated in its construction. The part that describes the construction process is noteworthy. We do not have time to read all of it, but here is one verse that is particularly striking: 'Truth cannot be seen; the sound of truth also cannot be heard because it rings throughout the universe. This bell was created so that all sentient beings can see and hear truth'. Then, the purpose of this bell is so that all who hear it can reach nirvana.

Now let's go over its physical characteristics. The bell is approximately 3.4 meters[11ft] tall, the diameter of the bottom is 2.3 meters[7.5ft] and the thickness is 2.4 centimeters[0.9in]. Its weight was unknown until very recently because there was no way to weigh the bell. There was no scale that could withstand this enormously heavy

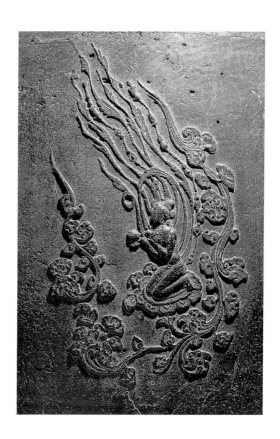

object. Finally in 1990 an electronic scale was produced that could support the weight of the bell and for the first time ever, an accurate weight measurement became possible. The resulting figure was 18.9 tons, meaning that the bell is a relatively heavy one.

Setting aside these figures for now, this bell is better known for its nickname Emile bell. The bell is said to be called the Emile bell because a child was thrown into the mixture of materials. The following is the story: In order to create the bell, money was forcibly extracted from the people. One person who could not afford this sum instead offered her child. The child was placed inside the bell. Afterwards, whenever the bell was rung there was a sound like a child calling for his mother, the source of the name Emile. But why did the story about a child in the bell spread at all? It probably came about to explain that phosphorus found in human bones was used to increase the cohesiveness of the metals, creating a strong alloy. Because of this, many people were highly curious as to whether elements of human bone are actually to be found in the bell. Incidentally, a substance examination was conducted at the same time that the bell was weighed that would clear up the entire situation. The result was completely different from the story that everyone had believed; no phosphorus traces were found in the alloy substance. Thus, the story that a child had been put into the bell turned out to be just that: a story.

Then why did this story come about in the first place? There were in fact situational factors at the time that contributed to the creation of the story. I believe that it came about because the process of making the bell was so difficult. It would not have been easy to create the greatest bell in the world. What kinds of difficulties were faced? Above all, an enormous amount of casting was required because of the size of the bell. In making the casting all at once, the key task was to prevent air bubbles from forming while cooling the material at the same time. This is said to be an extremely difficult task. If there are many air bubbles, there is an increased probability that the bell will crack and thus have a shorter lifespan as well as a variety of other problems. Because of the enormity of the task, it ends up taking many decades to create the bell. Perhaps this is why the gruesome legend of the child was able to come about.

A close examination of the bell also revealed that the bell did not have a consistent thickness. The results for the thickness of the top and bottom and the middle of the bell were different: what could have caused this? While the answer to this question was unknown before, cutting edge technology was able to provide the conclusive clue; we now know that the casting was created using highly advanced calculations. This is what allowed the bell's ring to be heard from even great distances away. Various technologies have been used in Korean bells to allow the sound to travel long distances; of these, the technique used for the Emile bell is said to have been the best.

The sound of Korean bells is famous for being able to be heard from very far away up to several kilometers. This is possible because of the beat phenomenon. It sounds a bit abstruse because it is a technical term, but the beat phenomenon basically refers to changing the frequency of the bell's ring. The two different frequencies of two sounds combine, forming an undulating pattern of weak and strong sound that allows it to travel farther. If you actually listen to a Korean bell, you will hear an 'oong-oong-oong' sound that repeats a pattern of dying out and becoming louder, the feeling of which lasts a long time after the ring has ended. In this way, the sound continues to propagate. The best application of this technology is said to be the Emile bell, the sound made possible by the different thicknesses of different parts of the bell. In other words, different frequencies are formed by each of the two thicknesses, which then combine together.

Given the limited knowledge of science technology at the tie, it is incredible how such advanced technology was discovered. The use of two different thicknesses in the bell is itself an amazing feat. But considering that the Emile bell is contemporaneous with Seokguram Grotto and Bulguksa, we can probably assume that technology was indeed advanced enough even so long ago. The creation of the Emile bell was possible because a world-class structure like Seokguram Grotto was able to be built around this time. But nevertheless it was an extremely difficult task, which is suggested in the sheer number of years that it took to complete the bell. The king who oversaw the creation of this bell was the same king who was in charge of Seokguram Grotto and Bulguksa; he died before the bell was completed. It was barely finished during the reign of his son, the next king. It took that many years to make a not-so-large bell. The entire process took at least a decade, a considerable portion of which must have been taken up by various trial-and-error attempts in using the various technologies that I have mentioned above. Upon measuring the frequency of the Emile bell, the first frequency came out to be 64Hz and the second frequency was 168Hz. Even the Japanese government-run television network NHK is said to have admitted that the Emile bell is the greatest bell in the world.

Some academics have even created a separate category for all Korean bells based on the Emile bell, known by the proper name 'Korean bell'. This attests to a unique device in Korean bells that differentiates them from others. Let's take a look at the explanation for this. It is present in the Emile bell as well: let's look at its top. You will see a small container encircled by a dragon. This container goes through the bell in a similar manner to a pipe and has the dual function of trapping extraneous sounds and spreading the sound across great distances. In other words, the container adjusts the tone of the sound so that it can spread out as far as possible. However, a recent study argues that the container has nothing to do with the bell's sound. The research is based on scientific measurements. If the results of this study are indeed correct, what is the function of this container? The dragon and container are said to be a representation of a popular legend at the time. It is very well-known in Korea, which basically states that a dragon presented the Silla king with a flute that would create peace all over the world by hearing its sound. According to scholars who study this legend, the container on top of the bell represents the Korean flute and the dragon is carrying it. From this perspective, the people of Silla hoped for world peace to occur by visually representing this legend on the bell.

In this way, it has been proven that the container on top of the bell has nothing to do with its sound. But the device at the bottom of the bell is clearly related to the sound. There is no question that it played a role in making the sound ring longer, because the sound formed inside the bell echoes more right at this spot. This device is not found in bells in China or Japan. There is no answer for why this device is only found in Korean bells but it is nonetheless clear that it is responsible for their unrivaled quality.

A German scholar is said to have declared after seeing the Emile bell that if a similar relic was found in his country, he would dedicate an entire museum just to that relic. I could not agree more with this opinion because as the bell with the most beautiful sound in the world, there is a need to spell out all the various secrets of this sound for everyone to know. Moreover, this task becomes even more crucial because we are no longer able to hear this bell live. Of course, it is still possible to hear the sound in the recordings that are sold in the museum souvenir shop. However, I believe that the sound could be heard more clearly with the technology of a good

• •

The Top and the Bottom of the Bell

sound system. Developments in virtual reality technology could also provide diverse opportunities of experiencing the bell, but I cannot know why this is not done.

While Koreans love to boast that it is the most beautiful bell sound in the world, they do not seem to care much about actually showing this off. Why else would this bell simply be hung in the museum courtyard for people to merely see? It is unfortunate that there is no way of enjoying the sound of the bell at any time you want under the best conditions for it. A recording of the sound is currently being played at intervals via loudspeakers, but this is wholly insufficient for conveying the full richness of the bell's ring. On one hand I receive the impression that there must be more relics in Gyeongju that are similar in level to the Emile bell, and that this bell is less of a priority than these. If there is still no official information center for a world-renown cultural relic like Seokguram Grotto, what hope can we have for the Emile bell?

Walking through the museum garden

If you walk around outside after having finished viewing the Emile bell, you will see that there are quite a few worthwhile relics to see. As we cannot see them all, let's discuss just a few. There is an interesting artifact close by the Emile bell that I always make sure to point out when I visit with my students. It is the foundation of a tombstone. A tombstone usually contains a description of the accomplishments of the person who is buried there, but this foundation is eye-catching. Most tombstone foundations are made with one turtle but this one has two. The occupant of the tomb must have had a high government office and the number of turtles was meant to show this off. This foundation is interesting because of the ornate and fancy necklaces carved on the necks of both turtles. I have seen countless tombstone foundations in my many trips, but have never seen one that uses two turtles with necklaces on them. It is most likely a reflection of Silla social custom at that time.

274

• •

The Tombstone Foundation at the Museum

      This work was probably created in the late eighth century, the golden age of Silla. Thanks to this, nobles at the time enjoyed unparalleled luxury; proof of this lies in the repeated orders by the king restricting the use of imported luxury goods. Among the list of forbidden items were: peacock tail feathers, turtle shells and a type of blue jewel from Tashkent. Peacocks were in India and parts of Southeast Asia while turtle shells were imported from Borneo or Java. Amidst such an era, the thought of putting necklaces on the necks of turtles may have seemed reasonable. It is similar to the way that we put expensive collars on the necks of domestic pets like puppies. Having fallen into an uncontrollable cycle of wealth consumption, the national defense power of Silla weakens by the day and eventually collapses at the beginning of the tenth century.

From these records we can see that Silla imported a great deal of items from other countries and had an active international trade system. This is supported by historical facts from that era showing that in the late eighth century there were millions of Silla people living in the Shandong province and over fifty thousand Arabs in Chang'an^{present-day Xi'an}, the capital of the Tang dynasty. There was a Silla individual named Chang Bogo who had a complete monopoly on sea trade and controlled the seas to such an extent that Japanese traders going to China could not help but to use his ships.

• • The Sassanid Persian Rock

There is evidence of this flourishing international trade in the yard of the museum that attracts our attention. In front of the Anapji exhibition hall, there is a strange rock as seen in the picture. You will see that there are designs of a tree, peacock and lion on the stone dating back to Sassanid Persia. On the far left is a circle with nothing inside it; it is likely that the stone was to be used in a construction project but later abandoned. As we can see here, there was so much trade going on that Silla nobles used Persian designs in their own homes.

This can be seen in what I discussed in the introduction of this book. A warrior statue found in front of a royal tomb area called Gwereung also proves this point. This tomb is on the outskirts of Gyeongju: the statue that we see here has the appearance of someone from Central Asia. The swarthy face, prominent muscles, tall height and the weapon in one hand lead to the assumption that it was some type of bodyguard. It is said that many Arab merchants lived near the Yangzi River and only took approximately one week to travel to Gyeongju from here by boat. Thus, Central Asians were easily able to come to Gyeongju through this water route and among these would definitely have been bodyguards of Silla royalty and nobility.

As long as we are walking around outside the museum, let's go in front of the Anapji exhibition hall. You will see two very familiar pagodas. These are Seokgatap and Dabotap, although they are of course replicas. It is common these days to recreate models of famous ancient relics, but I cannot fathom why there are replicas at a well-established national museum. A museum is supposed to be a place that displays real artifacts; I do not see how these replicas fit into this definition. It would have perhaps been understandable had they been used for educational purposes, but there are no such signs. Moreover, the Seokgatap replica looks awkward because its surface is smooth without the roughness of the bottom foundation as in the original. There are other errors to point out, but it is best to avoid replicas if at all possible.

If you go just next to this, you will see a dignified-looking pagoda as shown in the picture. This is unquestionably an original. It has the bearing of age which is very becoming. While such old objects are so wonderful, modern-day Koreans by contrast are unable to create anything that even comes close. All that then needs to be done is to stop making such objects, but the problem is that they are not aware of their shortcomings and keep creating strange things. This pagoda used to be in the yard of an ancient temple but was moved to this museum after the temple was destroyed. There is much to say about this eighth century pagoda, but what interests us here is its relationship to Seokgatap. To explain very briefly, while this pagoda is a work of art in and of itself, it can be seen as one part of the grand scheme of the history of stone pagodas in Korea to reach the final destination, Seokgatap.

A stone pagoda in Goseon-sa temple site Preserved in the courtyard of the Museum

I have already mentioned this in the chapter on Seokgatap, but Seokgatap is the greatest stone pagoda in Korea. This type of creation cannot come into being in just one try. There has to have been a process of development. The pagoda that is here at the museum is considered to be the one that came just before Seokgatap. Think of Seokgatap as the slimmed-down version of the pagoda that you see here. If you compare this with Seokgatap, you will see that the overall appearance matches exactly. Seokgatap took off the extra weight of this pagoda so that there would be nothing more to subtract. Of course, this does not detract from the beauty of this pagoda. Standing in front of this allows you to feel the valiant temperament of the people who lived back then.

Apart from this pagoda, there are many relics in the museum garden like Buddha statues and pagodas that require explanation. Let's be satisfied with glancing over the rest. It is impossible to see everything at a museum in one try; we will focus on what is important. We will now go inside the museum, but before we do so let's observe the line of Buddha images on the museum wall just in front of the pagoda as shown in the photograph. These Buddhas share one feature in common: they are all headless. I have already mentioned in an earlier section that this is most likely the result of Confucian believers who intentionally decapitated the statues in an attempt to shun Buddhism. Perhaps it was because the headless sight was unseemly that they were grouped in the back of the museum. Because of this, most visitors to the museum do not see them. I always bring my students to see these statues because some of them are actually of very good quality. I want my students to see not only the beauty of what is left of the statues but also the consequences brought about by provincial-minded Confucianists. I then make sure to point out that the stone Buddha at Bamian in Afghanistan was destroyed by the Taliban with the exact same principles.

● ●

Beheaded Buddha
Statues in the backyard
of the Museum

Inside Art Hall

Let us now really turn to the inside of the museum. There are three exhibition halls: Archaeology Hall, Art Hall, and Anapji Hall: we will be focusing on the first two because we have already discussed the artifacts excavated from Anapji. Let's first go to Art Hall because it is closer. The first thing you will notice when you go inside is the glass floor made so that you can see through it. What you see is a replica of a road from the Silla dynasty. This hall was newly built a few years ago and a Silla road was found in the construction process. This is a reconstruction of part of that road. A wagon has been created to match the wagon tracks on the road, and mannequins of the people who discovered the road add a realistic touch. In front of this is a miniature reproduction of Gyeongju 1000 years ago. Particularly attention-grabbing here is the nine-story Hwangnyongsa wooden pagoda. It is said that it could be seen from anywhere within downtown Gyeongju: this miniature model allows us to see what that must have looked like.

Befitting an art hall, there are many Buddhist relics on display. On the first floor there is a Buddha statue in front of which even those who are unfamiliar with Buddhist art are compelled to stop. The Buddha that is shown in this photo is called Baby Buddha because of its small size and its innocent expression. It cannot help

Baby Buddha Statues

being small because of the way that it is sitting. These three Buddhas are called the Three Maitreya Buddhas; they were moved here from Mount Nam. I will delete explanation of the Buddhist features, i.e. the middle Buddha is Maitreya, the significance of the hand gestures, etc. What is important is the appearance of these Buddhas. How would I express the aura of these Buddhas? Benevolent, soft, peaceful, friendly, etc. Even if I gather together all adjectives that describe purity and innocence, I would still not be able to properly describe the expressions on these faces. It forms a sharp contrast with the Buddha inside Seokguram Grotto. If the Buddha in Seokguram Grotto was very dignified, there is no dignity to be found in these Buddhas. They instead look very familiar and approachable. The bodhisattva's face on the right has the unaffected look of a child. The slightly forced smile even seems coquettish. The people of Silla did not think that Buddha was someone far away or on a high pedestal. They instead believed that Buddha had a friendly face and was an infinitely compassionate being who remained at their side. Looking at these Buddhas reminds me of the Buddha's face at the foot of Mount Nam because both are so naively innocent. The Buddha image traveled across Central Asia from India into China and Japan, but the somewhat nationalist thought occurs to me that none are so cute as the ones in Korea. This type of rustic Buddha is readily found in Korea. Because this reflects what people must have looked like at the time, I sometimes wonder whether all people in Silla back then were friendly and kindly people.

Of the many Buddhist relics in this building, the items that were discovered inside pagodas are worth viewing. An item found inside a pagoda refers to the box that holds the sarira; these are usually gold sculpted boxes on which very realistic and life-like looking people are carved. They are carved in bas relief and the technical skill used here is first-rate. But not all of the objects here are as fine and delicately made. There is a roof tile with a human face carved onto it that was found in the yard of a temple. You can see at first glance that it was not finely crafted. Roof tiles by nature cannot be finely crafted because they are printed out in bulk. However, the warm aura that exudes from this face makes it pleasant to look at. It is similar to what the Buddha statues that we have just seen look like. It is a nice face because it has no guile or artifice. However, only one such roof tile has been discovered thus far, and thus this particular tile is considered highly valuable even though a portion of it has chipped off. It may be merely a roof tile, but it is carefully displayed in its own section of the museum. People call this face the 'smile of Silla' and this face is always used when introducing Silla culture.

Another thing to note on this floor is the miniature replica of Hwangnyongsa. It is a very small depiction but you can still get a sense of its scale. You can also see how truly tall the nine-story wooden pagoda at its center really was. At that height, the fact that it was visible from anywhere in downtown Gyeongju seems very probable. I have already partially explained this pagoda in the section on Hwangnyongsa. But would this not occur to you about this pagoda?

I have said that this pagoda was built by artisans from Baekje, a nation that was more highly developed than Silla. If you look at the history of that period, there are many examples of such exchange; what is strange is how such exchange would have been

possible when Silla and Baekje were enemies. In front of this miniature Hwangnyongsa is displayed the restored roof tile that is the
only relic left of Dharma Hall. As you can see in the photo, this roof
tile is not so much a roof tile but one of the decorations that was
added to the edges of the roof. This type of large roof tile was used
to make the building look taller and more dignified. But because of
its length of 182 centimeters, we can see that it was divided into two
parts. Two roof tiles were combined together because it was difficult
to make a single roof tile this large. Observe the comic expression

on the human face in the middle of this tile. This type of humorous facial expression is also found in the clay figurines. Clay figurines are wonderful artifacts that give us insight into the common people's culture. These are displayed not in Art Hall where we are but in Archaeology Hall, the next-door building. This concludes our tour of Art Hall; let us now turn to Archaeology Hall.

At Archaeology Hall

Archaeology Hall was actually the main exhibition hall of this museum, but came to be called by its present name as more halls were added. We can see many of the relics that we discussed earlier in this book. Of these, 'jewelry sword' and the 'smiling pearl necklace' as seen in the photo are a feast for the eyes. The gold crown can also be seen at the National Museum of Korea, but the sword and necklace can only be seen here at the Gyeongju National Museum and so you should make sure to see these. The beauty of these objects when seen in person is truly dazzling. The highly decorated details on the sword and the life-like expression on the face on the pearl further draw our attention. As I have already explained these in the section on Daeneungwon, I will not explain them further here.

Beautiful Design of the Sword
©Gyeongju National Meseum

I did not discuss this earlier in the book, but if you look at the upper part of the sword you will see a beautiful design. There is no proven hypothesis on what this is supposed to symbolize and only various rumors. Some argue that it looks like a windmill while others argue that it looks like the sun. I do not know which of these explanations is correct. That is for scholars to decide: for us, it is enough to simply admire its beauty.

The relic that we truly need to focus on is in the next room. In this room we can see Silla as it was before advanced culture began being imported from China. We can get a glimpse of what the lives of common people must have been like without embellishment by Chinese or Confucian influence. The highlight of this room is the clay figurine to-u, literally dolls made of clay. It is nearly impossible to see these anywhere else in Korea. There are currently 350 such figurines left, and these were not discovered as part of the regular excavation but discovered nearby by chance. The most characteristic clay figurines are the ones on the surface of the clay pot as shown in the photo. These clay figurines cannot be listed as National Treasures because there are too many of them. Even now, these clay figures are discovered whenever there is a tomb excavation. There are so many that it is difficult to keep track and preserve them all. Thus, there is almost no instance of a clay figurine being registered as a National Treasure. But this clay figurine is registered as a National Treasure[No. 195]. Why is that? It is because there are figurines on the neck and upper part of this pot that are not found anywhere else. Thus, this pot is preserved in its own special glass compartment. Relics that are usually given this treatment are on the level of the gold crown; the fact that this pot is given its own compartment means that it is just as important as the crown. These figurines are usually discovered not in royal tombs but in those of the nobility. Thus, the design is not fitted to any sort of convention and is allowed to roam free.

The clay figurines on this pot are not only diverse but unique in form as well. The one that is on the front center is a figurine playing an instrument. The instrument looks a lot like the gayageum, a representative stringed traditional Korean instrument. If you compare it to the real gayageum, the top portion that is caved in on both sides is especially similar. But compared to the 12-stringed gayageum, the one being played by the figurine appears to have less strings; this may have been because the artisan simplified the object just so that it would generally look like the gayageum. Is the person playing the instrument a man or a woman? We cannot tell from the face but the protruding stomach means that it is probably a woman. Perhaps it has something to do with the explicitly crafted man and woman figurines right next to it engaged in sexual intercourse. It seems to express the fact that sexual intercourse leads to pregnancy, which would make the woman so happy that she is playing a musical instrument.

The defining characteristic of this pot is the couple engaged in intercourse; it is because of these two figurines that the pot has become a treasure. There is no other case in which a male and female figurine engaged in sexual intercourse were placed onto a pot. The scene is so explicit as to be embarrassing to the viewer. The male sex organ has been overly emphasized and the position itself is an extremely explicit one. As many children and minors visit the museum, it may be appropriate to prevent them from seeing this pot but there seems to be no restriction. It is said that the Japanese during the Japanese colonial period were so offended by these figurines that they took them off of the pot and preserved them elsewhere.

The standard explanation for the figurines engaged in sexual intercourse is the ancient importance placed on fertility. There is no doubt that fertility was extremely important to ancient societies. There are also animal figurines that symbolize fertility: the snake and frog. They are strangely positioned so that the snake has bitten

• • Clay Figurines on the Pot ©Gyeongju National Meseum

the back foot of the frog. We do not know exactly what the artist was trying to express here, but perhaps the many eggs laid by the frog was held up as the symbol of fertility. But fertility is not the only virtue that is symbolized. Figurines of the fish, bird and turtle are also present and it is clear that the turtle symbolizes longevity. The fish was an important staple of the diet at that time, and the bird can perhaps be seen as a messenger connecting heaven and earth although it was probably a food staple as well.

There is another clay figurine that should be noted in addition to this pot. These are the woman covering her mouth and a Central Asian. The Central Asian can be seen as a miniature version of the statue that we saw at Gwereung. We can conclude that foreigners were so prevalent that they were even made into clay figurines. The one that deserves more of our attention is the woman right next to it. This woman figurine is important for many reasons, one of them being that her clothing allows scholars to see what Silla people wore. Not only is it impossible for clothing from that period to have survived but there are almost no drawings that depict this; thus, the fact that this figurine shows an entire outfit makes it a priceless resource. We can also see the hairstyle and infer from it how women at that time styled their hair.

But this woman is covering her mouth with her hand, apparently because she is laughing. The expression has been depicted

• • The Clay Figurine of Smiling Woman ©Gyeongju National Meseum

by just a few lines but the life-like realism is astounding. It almost seems as if this woman is standing right in front of you. The fact that we know she is laughing just from her eyes and nose is amazing. This is the definitive feature of Silla clay figurines: they are not finely crafted nor are they detailed. They have been created with very simple hand movements and lines, but the depiction is always highly realistic. Minor details are deleted while important features are emphasized. The figurine of this naked female in the photo is one example of this. The face and other parts of the body are crudely created but the breasts and sex organ have been enlarged. There are many figurines on which the sex organs are heavily emphasized. This most likely has to do with conveying pleasure and fertility.

The way that these clay figurines capture one moment in time is also striking. The woman figurine that we just saw has captured her laughing by foregoing all minor details. The same technique is used for the face that we saw on the roof tile from Hwangnyongsa. This is the undecorated true appearance of ancient Silla people. In other words, this is what they looked like before the arrival of Chinese influence. These figurines look very simple, but artists today who are given this task are said to have difficulty recreating this look. Ones that are attempted today lack the breath of life that is present in the Silla figurines. But this type of artistic sensibility lasted well into the late Joseon dynasty. One example is this folk painting as shown in the picture. This tiger painting also deletes unnecessary details and emphasizes the parts that need to be emphasized to form an overall simple and comic image. In that sense, it is in the same class as the clay figurines of Silla.

Folk Painting of Tiger in the Joseon Dynasty

This concludes our tour of the museum. We did not visit the Anapji exhibition hall but you can go back to the section on Anapji to refresh your memory on what is here. There are many items on display that were used in daily life(i.e. scissors) as well as objects made for play like a dice and male sex organ. There are also materials that were used for buildings, allowing us to imagine what buildings back then may have looked like. An item that instantly grabs our attention is the boat in the middle of the room. It was found in the mud at the bottom of the pond, and is said to have been used to travel around the pond and enjoy the scenery. It was able to preserve this much of its original appearance because the soft mud slowed down the rotting process. It is almost unbelievable that this boat is over 1000 years old. After one last look at this room, let us now leave the museum.

Afterword:

BETWEEN DEVELOPMENT & PRESERVATION

We have covered many of Gyeongju's most important relics in our tour, but there is a great deal more that we did not have a chance to see. Also, there is a promise I made at the beginning of this book that I did not keep. Because it is impossible to see all of the relics in Gyeongju, I promised that we would only see those that are registered under UNESCO. But there is one UNESCO relic that we did not see: Myeonghwal Fortress is approximately a 30~40 minute drive away from eastern Gyeongju. While this is an important site for Korean history majors, it does not hold much significance for non-experts. There is also nothing artistically outstanding about this fortress. It has no greater significance apart from the fact that was the fortress guarding Gyeongju. I do not know why it was been registered as a UNESCO heritage item and I myself have never visited Myeonghwal Fortress. For these various reasons, Myeonghwal Fortress was not included in this book.

If there are places in the world that make you feel good simply by visiting them, Gyeongju is definitely included. Gyeongju is a place that even if you have visited last week, you find yourself wanting to go again this week. This is probably why the people of Silla did not move their capital city for 1000 years and chose to remain in a rather secluded part of the peninsula. Gyeongju is a special place. But as with any ancient city, it endured a great deal of hardship caught between the needs of preservation and modern development and continues to suffer from this today. Gyeongju began to acquire its current looks beginning with the 10-year development plan of 1971 begun under President Park Chung Hee, a famous dictator as well as the leader who is responsible for the economic 'miracle of the Han'. Bomun Complex, the largest tourist complex in Gyeongju today, was also created under the Park administration. There seem to be heavily conflicting opinions on this period of development. Academia criticizes this development period as 'systematic destruction that is worse than grave robbing'. There is also the evaluation that Gyeongju was able to upgrade itself as a city thanks to the development that occurred at this time. An example of the destruction is the 1990 Jugong Apartment incident, in which ironware relics from the third century were discovered inside Jugong Apartment complex but restoration of these relics was given up on. I am sure that the government, city construction agency, Gyeongju citizens and academics each have their own position in incidents like these. But current policies do not seem to satisfy any one of these interest groups.

If asked my opinion on this issue, I am tempted to argue that what is old should always be preserved no matter what. Old artifacts may seem unimportant now, but nobody knows what may happen in the future. Who knows whether a certain artifact will suddenly become valuable, whether for academic purposes or tourism? This is why I believe that having an unconditional preservation policy for relics and historic sites is the smart thing to do for the sake of future generations. If this is not considered at all and destroyed today, there is no way of undoing the damage later. Cultural heritages by nature need to be preserved with utmost care.

Perhaps this explains why the Gyeongju that I saw in 1964 before development projects began is the most beautiful memory that I have of the city. I was only in third grade at the time, but the Gyeongju that I saw then remains a much better memory than the Gyeongju that I have seen on countless subsequent field trips. For example, while major relics and historic sites are arguably the main assets of Gyeongju, the beauty of its natural surroundings is also just as valuable. The homey feeling that I get whenever I visit Gyeongju is probably due to the latter, and it truly grieves me to see the nature continuously be sacrificed in the name of development. I especially bemoan the sudden and unannounced entry of large apartment complexes. They say that there are currently approximately 500 apartment complexes in the Gyeongju area; this figure will most likely continue to increase and not decrease. Citizens of this city probably wish to improve living quality by moving into shiny new apartments, but I still become upset when I see that the old look of the city continues to disappear.

Gyeongju citizens probably have a lot to say as well. It is easy for them to make slight adjustments to their homes, but it is extremely difficult to rebuild old homes or build new ones. This is because of legal restrictions. Predictably, houses do not sell very well. Moreover, if a relic is discovered in the construction or reconstruction process, it is literally the end for that home because excavation costs must be covered by either the construction company or the home owner. If a construction company discovers an artifact while digging up the ground to build a new apartment complex, it is a given that the company will come close to bankruptcy. As such, cultural heritage laws in Korea are first and foremost made to benefit the government. Then is there no solution at all? The best way is for the government to purchase land that has many relics in it, guarantee the aftercare of these relics and keep track of them in a systematic manner. But as always, these efforts are hampered by budget shortages. The Gyeongju city government began purchasing a massive 3000 acre plot in 1998 as a protected area, but it has not yet been resolved because it costs what would have been 2 trillion won in 1998. The fact that tombs that contain many gold relics are properly excavated while there are no records of ordinary home lots being investigated is a telling piece of evidence. As of 2009, there is a district near Gyeongju Station called Jjoksaem District that is being excavated. It is said to be a relatively small site, but even this will take 50 years to finish purchasing. There is no way of knowing how cultural relics in Gyeongju will be investigated and kept track of in the future.

300

Such debates concerning the preservation and development of Gyeongju have always been around. Whatever the right solution is, I strongly recommend that the city of Gyeongju be transformed into the most ideal cultural tourism site in Korea. How will this be achieved? As an academic, the first task would obviously be proper investigative research on all cultural relics. From the perspective of tourism, I would say that the city should be made so that from the moment that tourists set foot in Gyeongju, the city should look and feel like another world. In other words, those who visit Gyeongju should feel so connected to the old culture and natural surroundings of this city that they forget that they live in the twenty-first century. This is especially crucial for Gyeongju because it was one of the four great ancient cities of the world. One thing that must be avoided is the hurried construction of 'tourism complexes' and restaurants in these areas. The city must be redesigned so that it recovers as much of its original appearance as possible. More tourists visit Gyeongju to see relics than to simply rest and relax. Everything must be redone so that such people can feel a unique Buddhist atmosphere that they are unable to find in any other city in Korea. All of this will of course require a great deal of funding; the most important task here is to gather peoples' opinions. I can only hope that people who truly love Gyeongju can find one another and together find the best possible resolution.

Author _ Choi Joon-Sik Ph.D.

Professor Choi earned his B.A. degree in Korean History from
Sogang University, Korea and received his Ph.D. degree in
Religious Studies from Temple University in Philadelphia in 1988.
He has held the position of Professor of Korean Studies at Ewha Womans
University since 1992. His research interests are religious studies, and
socio-cultural studies and arts of Korea. He is currently the director of Korea
Culture Rearch Institue at Ewha Womans University.

Translator _ Sandra Choe

Sandra Choe received her B.A. in English at Wellesley College and
in currently pursuing an M.A. in Korean Studies at Yonsei University.
She has also translated *Seoul: A Window into Korean Culture*.

Gyeongju
The Heart of Korean Culture
A UNESCO World Heritage

First Published in May 2011

Published by Hanul Publishing Group
Head office _ 535-7, 302, Gyoha-eup, Munbal-ri, Paju-si, Gyeonggi-do, 413-756
Seoul office _ 105-90, 1F Seoul Bldg., Gongdeok-1dong, Mapo-gu, Seoul, 121-801

Tel. 82-31-955-0606, 82-2-326-0095 | Fax. 82-2-333-7543
Homepage. www.hanulbooks.co.kr

ISBN 978-89-460-5351-9 03900(Hardcover)
        978-89-460-4434-0 03900(Paperback)

Printed and bound in the Republic of Korea.